OLD KETTERING
– A VIEW FROM
THE 1930s

Book 5

For Bessie

– every good
wish, + happy

memories

Tony Ireson

10 · xi · 97

OLD KETTERING – A VIEW FROM THE 1930s

Book 5

TONY IRESON

Published by the author and printed by
Woolnough Bookbinding Ltd
Irthlingborough, Northamptonshire

1997

ISBN 0 9509800 5 6

By the same author:

NORTHAMPTONSHIRE
  Robert Hale County Books
  1954, reprints 1954, 1955, 1960
  New edition 1964, reprints 1968, 1969
  New edition 1974

OLD KETTERING AND ITS DEFENDERS
  1984, 1991 with postscript

OLD KETTERING – A VIEW FROM THE 1930s Book 1
  1988, 1991

OLD KETTERING – A VIEW FROM THE 1930s Book 2
  1990, 1992

OLD KETTERING – A VIEW FROM THE 1930s Book 3
  1992

OLD KETTERING – A VIEW FROM THE 1930s Book 4
  1994

Typeset in 10/12pt Melliza by Woolnough Bookbinding, Irthlingborough, Northamptonshire

CONTENTS

ILLUSTRATIONS

Frontispiece shows Kettering on a summer afternoon in 1960, before the planners seized upon it. Dr. Roughton's miniature forest in Northampton Road was still there, the cattle market was in use, the Grammar and High Schools were sharing their Bowling Green Road building, and the old police station, the courts, and the Parish Church School were standing. Gold Street was intact, the Electricity Works dominated Rockingham Road, and Timpson's factory loomed in the distance. A time fondly remembered.

(Picture: Evening Telegraph, then in Dryland Street for 63 years).

I love everything that's old: old friends, old times, old manners, old books, old wine.
– Oliver Goldsmith in 'She Stoops to Conquer.'

INTRODUCTION

Like the walls of Jericho, buildings that were once busy factories continue to come tumbling down. Latest are William Timpson's, exchanged for houses, Freeman Hardy and Willis supplanted by Dove Court, and others large and small removed or adapted for houses or flats. I use the old names because that is how the buildings are remembered.

This alteration of the town scene is the outward sign of fundamental change. The frontispiece of this book was taken to mark the moment when Kettering was about to lose its self-sufficiency and become, for good or ill, subject to the pressure of external influences.

Since then old Kettering has gone. No longer do we hear the factory starting sirens, or see the early morning foot-and-bike brigade hurrying to work, to be locked out and lose pay if late. Except for girl shoe-closers who managed a touch of brightness, the operatives were deliberately shabby, for though clothing work was clean many shoe and leather jobs were not, so oldest clothes and footwear broken down by pedal-pounding were the rule. The factory doors closed behind them, and after an interval white collar workers and pupils making for school brought a colourful touch to the street scene. They were all individuals, greeting and waving to one another, for the only people who went to work by car in those days were heads of firms bound for executive desks.

Regardless of station, those were all remarkable men and women who, by hand or brain or both, fashioned Kettering during its industrial struggles. In comparatively primitive times they fought against odds at work and at home, and by sheer grit created a town to be proud of and a fine place to live in.

It was always a friendly town, and still is. Kettering's historic products – shoes, clothing and engineering – laid their stamp on people. Anyone's name, job and address provided an instant mental impression of them in a community where within limits everyone knew everyone else because they were linked by work, businesses, churches, extended families, or the arts and hobbies, which were pursued with enthusiasm and often distinction cutting across social barriers.

Today these personal links are weaker. People who once knew everybody in their street now look out on passing strangers. In part it is due to the disappearance of the old staple trade factories, reduced to a handful making shoes and clothing. In place of the old firms that have gone, a diversified range of enterprises large and small has sprung up. Apart from notable exceptions, many are not distinctively local, but are integrated with the rest of the country because of Kettering's excellent communications. Increasingly people want to live in Kettering because of its advantages, and work elsewhere, or they find jobs in the town and come in each day. Because of its still welcoming charm and friendliness, Kettering has a magnetic attraction.

Considerable prosperity has accompanied new developments in every field, as is evident from the amount of trade done in the major establishments. Yet there are problems. One is concealed poverty. In 1996 the Council named two wards that needed upgrading. It wanted Government help in training youngsters, setting up youth employment, supporting health campaigns and anti-crime measures, and providing new housing and community facilities. Another problem is the migration of businesses from the town centre, leaving vacant sites and empty shops.

Vacant land in the town centre needs to be built upon before any more green fields are sacrificed, yet three major schemes for the use of town centre land envisage the building of shops, some under planning decisions made many years ago. If these views were relaxed to permit the natural development of suitable areas it might be that housing, offices and light industry would wish to in-fill. This would bring residents and workers into the town centre, able to do shopping in the central streets to the benefit of run down areas. The appointment of a town centre manager shows that it is not a simple problem.

Meanwhile, discussion of our present-day problems of affluence must not blot out memories of earlier days, less than a lifetime ago, which contrast unbelievably with today when we have so many blessings at the turn of a switch, and incalculable benefits in the fields of medicine and personal freedom. It is a far cry to some of the blighted lives our great-grandparents witnessed. Wounded Great War ex-Servicemen ekeing out a living in the streets. Homeless tramps illegally cadging tea and scraps at back doors before trudging the dozen miles to the next casual wards where they got a meal, bath and bed before doing some work and being sent off again. Clergymen visiting the poor and sick, and sometimes leaving coins on the table. Shoeless children. Busy pawnbrokers. And for the poorest a last refuge in the dreaded workhouse and a pauper's funeral. Life can still be cruel, but perhaps less callously than in the between-wars decades.

In those days there seemed to be little misbehaviour or crime. The law was ever-present to catch up with wrongdoing, right down to bikes-without-lights, and people felt safe both indoors and out. There were savage penalties for major offences, from the birch or prison with hard labour to the hangman's noose. I have tried to recapture the macabre fascination of murder trials in those days with a full version of the Rouse story. He was hanged for the 'blazing car murder', although those who fought to save him claimed that the jury could not have had open minds. The full story makes fascinating reading.

It was a relief to turn from that tragedy to the sporting sagas of old Kettering, which so often fielded teams to be reckoned with. I have told stories about the town's cricket, soccer and rugby clubs which are necessarily all-male except for an attempt at ladies' cricket at Rushton, and the dominating figure of 'Ma' Evans at the Royal who for years reigned over the social and domestic side of the Rugby Club. Sadly, I unearthed the story of a fatal accident at cricket.

It was a pleasure to record some of the achievements of the old urban council. Towns had to look after themselves before the health service and other national dispensers of life's basic needs came on the scene, and local people rose splendidly to shoulder at times awesome responsibilities. For example, dealing with the dreadful drought of 1934 when Kettering all but ran out of water, and we had to drink the Wicksteed Lake. I found myself moved by the wonderful descriptions of church services and activities from people who were youthful worshippers. What may we lose if churchgoing passes out of our regular observance of the passage of time, great events, and the cycles of Nature?

I hope you enjoy the book. Its object is to pay tribute to those whose contribution to our prosperous and growing town must never be forgotten. It has been great to remember so many of them, and I am sure that just reading their names will spark off more memories.

My warmest thanks to all who have helped by so kindly bringing me information, tolerating my phone calls, and discovering or taking photographs. Contributions are acknowledged in the text, but those whose helpfulness was behind the scenes and needs special mention are Anne Weightman for her research at national sources, Frank Thompson who lent me his cuttings and essays, and Malcolm Robinson at the Public Library. Should you detect mistakes and omissions, there is only one person to blame . . .

TONY IRESON
Kettering, 1997

GRASS ROOTS

Since Book 4 was published lots of people have come back or been in touch to pick up where they left off. Trendsetters were the shoemaking Easts who gave us Sir Alfred, knighted in 1910 as England's greatest living landscape artist. His great-great-nephew Frederick who lives in Devon found that the history books attribute the wrong birth year to Alfred who first saw the light on 15 December 1844, not 1849, in the corner house to Gold End and Lower Street, now gone.

Frederick advised the Art Gallery, and to mark the correct date an Alfred East exhibition was arranged for the 150th anniversary of his birth. At the opening were family and friends, among them Martin Taylor who is writing a biography of Sir Alfred and painting modern versions of the scenes he loved. It was found that a gravestone had never been erected to the artist's parents, Benjamin and Elizabeth East, and a stone to mark the spot was added just inside the north gate of London Road Cemetery.

Next to return, on 23 March 1995, were the Drylands, for the unveiling of the restored Dryland Memorial, erected by public subscription in 1907 to Dr. John Winter Dryland. He was so beloved that even widows in Sawyer's Almshouses and 'paupers' in the workhouse who came under his care asked permission to contribute. Those were days of thirsty pedestrians, cyclists, horses and dogs, and towns with money were erecting horse troughs and drinking fountains, often splendid works of art.

Kettering followed suit, remembering Dr. Dryland with the memorial at the front of the Library, designed by J. A. Gotch to complement the building. It is a richly carved and inscribed central pillar flanked by troughs, with a drinking fountain for passers-by and a ground level bowl for dogs. It lost its use, though not its interest and value to the scene when horses gave way to motors, and in 1947 it was officially vandalised when a council mandarin ordered destruction of the troughs. This senseless action was to make room for more bus shelters of tubular steel with plastic roofs.

One virtue of the shelters was that they were easily removable, but when they were demolished the central pillar of the memorial was left for many years lonely, pointless, battered and forlorn.

In time a conservation order was placed on the area which includes the parish church, public library, manor house museum, art gallery, almshouses, gardens, the municipal offices, the historic London Road cemetery, and as a final touch one of the old red telephone boxes. In sympathy with this the Civic Society determined to get the memorial restored. It raised funds and enlisted support from the Borough Council, County Council and Anglia Water for new troughs to be made and reunited to the central pillar by stonemason Keith Wright of Islip and architect Paul Ansell so that the memorial re-emerged in pristine perfection.

The widely-scattered Drylands supported the project with enthusiasm and Professor Katherine Dryland Vig of Ohio State University came to unveil the restored memorial to her great-grandfather. She was welcomed by mayor Eric Bellamy-Tall, Dr. Peter McCormick of the Dryland medical practice and Dr. Robert Wigglesworth, Civic Society president.

After the ceremony the company moved across to the George Hotel for an informal lunch. Among the guests, traced by Civic Society chairman Arthur Heath, was Kenneth Mitchell of Aldwincle who 40 years earlier on orders from above had been obliged to sledge-hammer the original troughs. It was appropriate that soon after this official act of atonement Arthur Heath was appointed MBE in recognition of 25 years' work for conservation.

At the gathering I had the pleasure of meeting Geoffrey Dryland who as a captain in the Cheshire Yeomanry, the last British Regiment to fight on horseback, rode in a cavalry charge in the last war against the Vichy French. He confirmed that the old cavalry horse I mentioned in Book 2 would have recognised bugle calls though harnessed to a civvy street cart.

Third family among the returning pilgrims were the Gotches, who came in force on 21 April 1995 for the opening of the Magic Web exhibition of pictures by Thomas Cooper Gotch. More than 50 Gotch descendants stayed at the Royal Hotel in which 190 years earlier when it was the White Hart a meeting to decide how Kettering should help to resist an anticipated Napoleonic invasion was chaired by Thomas Gotch, the town's shoe manufacturing pioneer and acknowledged leader.

Ages of Gotches from all over the country ranged from brothers Paul and Christopher in their seventies down to the youngest aged one. Besides visiting the exhibition and a display at the museum showing the contribution of the Gotches to the town they were taken by Mrs. Dye on a tour of Chesham House, once the family residence which had become social services offices.

Paul reflected "We all enjoyed our visit. It gave the family new knowledge of our historic links with Kettering, and its people an awareness that our family is still very interested in the well-being of this fine market town from which our forebears came."

Among many personal flashbacks Jack Carter, who lives at Neath, gave me vivid impressions of Operation Harpoon, the convoy which relieved Malta in June 1942 (Book 4). He was a Royal Artillery gunner in the merchant ship *Burdwan*, and after she was disabled and sunk he was rescued by *HMS Badsworth*, commanded by Lieutenant (later Rear Admiral) Gray, grandson of John Elworthy, the Kettering brewer.

Jack said "I joined the *Burdwan* at Swansea docks and was given a less than cheerful greeting by her master. 'This ship isn't coming back' he said. When the convoy of six merchant ships was bombed nearing Malta *Burdwan* was the fourth to be hit. We had to abandon ship, and got on to *Badsworth* by rope ladders. We were in her forepart when she hit a mine, and I got out through a hole in the deck. You remember some strange things. The lascar seamen always kept their belongings strapped to them, and one was picked up with his alarm clock slung round his neck." A watercolour of *Badsworth* in her wartime camouflage, painted by Rear Admiral Gray, has been presented to the Art Gallery.

Syd Smith, Naval gunner on the merchant ship *Baltonia*, sunk off Gibraltar in 1943, has had friendly contact with crew members of German submarine *U118*, which did the damage, and with George Hicks and Jake Warren of the Canadian corvette *Alberni* which picked him up from the sea. Jake, who became Canadian High Commissioner in London 1971-75 says "I always remember that ship going down. I was in charge of the port boat picking up survivors, and it was a weird experience. We were pulling literally through a sea of oranges intended to meet the needs of citrus-starved Britain." The oranges floated free when *Baltonia* struck one of *U118's* mines.

On leave, Syd was invited to a board meeting of the *Evening Telegraph*, on which he worked, was given the place of honour, and after describing his ordeal was presented with £10 – real money then – by Sir Richard Winfrey, head of the outfit . The cash was to buy a new watch, as in the action Syd lost an inscribed gold watch given him by his father, who had carried it on the Western Front in the 1914 war. Syd had lent it to another member of the gun crew, whom he never saw again, but eventually the watch was returned through the Admiralty. George Hicks told Syd "Captain Ian Bell sent the belongings of the dead men we picked up back to their relatives in England. Your watch was found on the deck." It still keeps perfect time.

Alberni and *U118* were both sunk later. The corvette went down in 30 seconds after being hit by an acoustic torpedo, and the submarine was blown to pieces trying to fight it out on the surface with nine circling US bombers.

Jack Kendall of Brentwood sent me a story about A. J. Wright, MC and DSO at Gallipoli, who after the first war taught maths at Wellingborough School. Of the Kettering shoemaking and sporting family, he was a brilliant teacher held in affection and respect by the boys. Their regard took a practical form every day, for AJ always spent his lunch break in the Hind and stayed until closing time, which meant that he returned to school a quarter of an hour late to take his afternoon class. But none of the boys ever spoke about this, and if the rest of the teachers knew they turned a blind eye.

Jack is researching one of his tribe, Robert Kendall who was hanged on Northampton Racecourse on 13 August 1813 for robbing the Leeds mail on 26 October 1812. That evening the coach, bound for London, called at Kettering post office in George Street and picked up letters and packets from postmistress Sarah Stockburn.

At Burton Latimer the driver stopped to light the lamps, and went on through Finedon, where the guard climbed over to sit with him. When they changed horses at the Green Dragon, Higham Ferrers they found the rear locker broken open and the mail stolen. The job had been neatly done by someone jogging behind as the coach slowed uphill at Finedon, where discarded letters were found.

Suspicion fell on Robert Kendall who lived with his sister Mary at Bythorn. Earlier on the day of the robbery he had driven his cart to Finedon carrying as a passenger Huffey White, a notorious criminal. The two were together in the Woolpack, Islip, before the robbery and in Wellingborough after it. A few days later Mary and White went off to London together and lived in style, drawing attention to themselves by passing high-value notes. With Robert Kendall they were arrested and charged with the robbery.

At the trial in Northampton Mary was acquitted, but White and Kendall were sentenced to death. White told the judge that Kendall never knew of his intention to rob the mail, but this did not save him because he could not account for his movements on the evening of the crime.

The double hanging attracted the largest crowd ever seen at a public execution on the racecourse, and gave rise to a scandal which lasted for weeks. When the two were handed over to the hangman Kendall was drunk, and loudly protested his innocence, though told to shut up by Huffey White. Drunkenness at such a moment horrified puritan opinion, and a magistrate held an official inquiry. It seemed that Kendall had received the Sacrament at a service before leaving prison, and then someone gave him the communion wine to finish up. Everyone kept their own counsel, and no scapegoat was detected. Huffey White was such a slippery customer that he several times escaped from custody, even when in the 'hulks', and it was on record that he once proved to Mr. Gotch that he had broken into the bank and gone through papers, but did not steal anything.

Mrs. Rita Gray, writing from Eastbourne, recalled Ivy's Cafe in the passage linking Gold Street and Silver Street. Rita, maiden name Nursey, lived in Nelson Street and married professional ballroom dancing champion Allan Gray who opened a school of dancing over Ivy's, then run by Mr. Exley. Allan is also remembered as MC at the George Hotel's Saturday night dancing to Tom Ashby's Band. Rita's father William was a bespoke tailor in Hampden Crescent who did alterations to Clark Gable's uniforms during the war. The star autographed a picture of Rita's sister Norma which William had in his wallet.

Rita went from Park Road to the High School, bought a bike

from Garley's in Regent Street, and on the way home used to drop in at the Victoria Picture House where her mother worked taking tickets: "I delighted in seeing the silent film stars. Mother told me later that a colleague of hers was Mrs. Calvert who used to take young Eddie with her to work in a clothes basket, and left him in the dressing room until the performance was over:

"Could Eddie Calvert's mother have been the saxophone and clarinet player Ada you mention in your description of the old 'Vic'? I read that Eddie is still entertaining with his golden trumpet in the North of England."

Rita worked in the Kaycee offices, but had to move to the factory when she married, as only single women were eligible for office jobs. She learnt to sew, and started as a machinist in 1933 at 8s 3d a week. Brother Frederick and sister Norma live in Kettering, and sister Edna died in 1986.

Charles Mason contributed a sad footnote about the demise of the 'Vic' orchestra which for years accompanied silent films and gave concerts in the intervals. Charles was a violin pupil of Pierre de Chaine, the last leader of the orchestra. When a Peterborough cinema installed talkies, Charles drove Pierre and some of the players over to see and hear the new marvel: "The outward journey was a lively trip in my father's bullnose Morris, everybody joking about talking films and saying they would just be a nine days wonder, but coming back was very different, everyone sad and dejected. They knew that silent films were finished, and that their jobs would vanish overnight."

Mrs. Phyllis Purdy of Northampton told me that in the Library is a secret memorial to the men who built it. When the tablet commemorating donors of the site was fixed, the workers sealed a group photograph of themselves behind it. Mrs. Purdy's father Ernest Woolmer was one of the bricklayers who carried out the excellent construction work. Another of his jobs was pointing the stonework of the parish church turrets and battlements. Scorning scaffolding, he was suspended by his mates trowel in hand to apply the mortar.

With Fred Moore, Phyllis put me right about the picture of a big gathering on Market Place in Tony Smith's *Kettering Revisited* which I suggested showed a service of intercession at a critical wartime juncture in 1917. They both identify it as a gathering to honour Sergeant William Boulter after he won the VC at Trones

Wood. He is visible on the platform, and Mrs. Purdy as a child was present.

She mourns a magnificent wistaria which grew along the frontage of the George Hotel.

Mrs. Nora Smith wrote about Benjamin Mitton who died aged 87 on 18 November 1897. Born at the tollgate house on Rothwell Road, kept by his father, he became landlord of the Woolpack in Horsemarket (now Henry's), started a weaving business behind it, and was also a fishmonger. He laid out Mitton's bowling green, on the corner of London Road and Bowling Green Road, which proved highly popular especially at the Feast when Ben built seats for the band in the branches of a big tree.

The green had a long history for when in 1879 the Local Board bought it from the Watsons of Rockingham Castle it was described as the old bowling green "where for centuries have met natives and friends upon the annual Feast of St. Peter to join in games and dancing." On the site the Local Board established the cattle market, spending £8,000 on the land and market rights, including buildings and pens for 800 cattle and 1,400 sheep.

Ben laid out another green adjoining his house in London Road. He had sons William and Alfred and a daughter, Mrs. Breakspeare, by his first wife, Miss Elkin, and one daughter, Mrs. Barker, by his second wife. Ben was the great-great-grandfather of Phil Smith, Nora's husband.

Jean Groome (née Daisy Worth) reflected from Watford: "Kettering was such a settled place in the '30s and '40s. Arriving from Toronto was a culture shock for us. Everyone there had the latest gadgets, but when my mother mentioned in Kettering that she was used to having a washing machine she was told that only lazy people needed them. The High School inculcated good manners. We had to change from outdoor to indoor shoes, with prefects to check, and school lunch was an occasion, the teachers at high table and the girls in groups with a senior in charge. Grace was said, and no one might start until permission was given. Uniform was strictly observed, and we were told that before the war it included white gloves.

"There was a sense of order and tradition. Last year I heard that Wilkie (Miss Wilkinson, English teacher) had died in her nineties. She was small, perhaps only five feet, and from the lower fourth onwards was passed in stature by all the girls. But she had an outsize personality, and could throw chalk or a blackboard rubber without hitting anyone but waking us up. 'No one sleeps in my classes,' she used to say.

"She made English grammar exciting, and her favourite practical was to bring in an armful of national newspapers and set us the task of finding grammatical mistakes and common errors." Among Daisy's contemporaries were Jean Thurgar, Pamela Curtis, Sonia and Anita Seddon, Pamela Collinrose, Gladys Tilley and Margaret Godfrey, and at KGS were David Green, fast bowler for Northants for a time, and Dickie Dyson.

From Mary Kennett of Langstone, Gwent, came an amusing tale about her grandfather Peter Hunt. Peter made Royal Hunt pedal bikes, owned Kettering's first motor car, and taught people to ride bicycles on a track beside his house, 74 Montagu Street. He was commissioned to teach the Duchess of Buccleuch and went to Boughton House to give the lessons.

Scenting some amusement, the Duke stood by to savour the spectacle, but things were not going well and the duchess and terra firma seemed likely to make painful contact. Says Mary, describing the scene "Father was apparently rather wary, but the Duke shouted 'Grab her round the waist, man!' and he did."

Mary's mother Freda Hunt married Tommy Macgill, one of the Poppies' star players between the wars. He went on to play for Charlton, then joined Lovells of Newport who won the Southern and Welsh leagues several times, and was trainer after he finished playing. Mary adds: "Although father was quite a wizz on the football field, he was not so able on the dance floor, and we were forever being told the story of how he once fell into the drum."

A telephone call asking when gas was first made in Kettering set me reflecting on the problems of the pioneers. Kettering Gas Company was founded in 1833, nearly a quarter of a century before the railway came, so that coal supplies were brought in by road in all weathers, a challenging horse transport job. The coal came first by canal to Market Harborough, the nearest transhipment point, and sometimes by rail to the nearest unloading bay at Thrapston. I heard that when the Gas Company was nationalised the records were not handed over with the works, and were destroyed, except for the first annual report.

I wonder whether any of the others may have survived? They would form a rich vein for students. The town depended on gas for light and power in pre-electricity days when gas engines drove factory machinery, but horse transport for the coal was the essential foundation of the whole process. The thought of negotiating the old Clack Hill with horses in frosty weather almost gives one heart failure.

Now for a minor mystery. In Book 4 I said that the tree surrounded by railings and seats which grew for many years on an island at the top of Bowling Green Road was an oak. John Pemble, in whose care the tree reposed when he was parks superintendent says it was a lime. Pat Wallis, researching her family, found the tree recorded as an oak on page 25 of a volume of newspaper cuttings in the Public Library. It was planted by John Walis in 1887 to mark Queen Victoria's golden jubilee. John Pemble estimated that his lime was planted about 1913. So unless one species can change into another and Darwin missed out, it seems that the oak didn't like its surroundings and died, to be replaced by a more town-tolerant lime. Come to think of it, I never noticed any acorns lying around. What happened to the medal and coins planted at the foot of the original tree?

A poignant spectacle during summer 1996 was the disappearance from the corner of Bath Road and Burghley Street of the former Timpson factory, for more than 70 years the flagship of the Kettering shoe manufacturing industry. Designed by architect R. J. Williams, it was an early example of a concrete frame building, permitting big windows giving maximum light to the operatives, and adorned with superimposed brickwork to harmonise with the town scene.

It supplied the national chain of Timpson shops, controlled from an adjacent office block, and the firm had moved upward under William Timpson, its founder, from a shed in his garden in Station Road via another factory behind Market Street. Opening of the Bath Road works was signalled in 1922 by a party for 1,000 on the premises, with Tom Mursell, Frank Wright, Ernest Woodcock and George Chester as principal speakers. Output was 7,000 pairs a week, and the inclusion of ladies' footwear brought a new branch of the industry to Kettering. Through two generations the factory helped to bring prosperity to the town under the wing of the family, and the gradual severence of links was sad, though it stimulated many memories. For example social change was illustrated by Sybil Skinner of Desborough recalling that at one time female staff were referred to as 'office ladies', 'factory girls', and 'cleaning women'. New houses sprang up on the site, and few relics of the factory are left. I have two. The young lady in reception had to work the phone exchange and deal with callers. She had her back to the entrance door, and a mirror hung over the switchboard so that she could see who was coming in. Glad to say, I picked up the mirror and an executive bookshelf at a sale. Rubble from the factory – 1,000 tons of it – went to make hardstanding of the car scrapyard on the site of the former Cransley Furnaces. Sic transit . . !

In my young-reporter days it was a blacklist error to confuse in print Timpsons the shoe firm with Timsons the engineers, also in Bath Road but spelt without a 'p'. Starting from a cellar in Victoria Street, Timsons have become the crowning development of the old-established Kettering engineering industry, and are world-famous as makers of printing presses.

A photograph has survived of the workers over 100 years ago at Owen Robinson's engineering works. Among them are Arthur Timson, standing, clean shaven and cloth capped, Charles Barber also standing and cloth capped, with a splendid moustache, and Charles Bullock, then one up as he was seated and wore an impressive homburg hat in addition to an even more splendid moustache and a gold watch and chain.

Arthur Timson left Robinsons to start repairing shoe machinery, bicycles and motor cycles in his parents' cellar. He prospered, invited the other two to join him, and they gradually built up the business of Timson, Bullock and Barber, undertaking engineering work of all types. It became Timsons Ltd. in 1934.

Only excellence was good enough, proclaimed by the title of the works – Perfecta. The premises gradually extended on both sides of Bath Road, through the 1930s producing printing presses made to the requirements of each individual customer. Orders spread through the Empire, into European countries, and eventually to the USA.

In the 1930s when output averaged 24 presses a year, *Punch* and *Hansard* were printed on Timson presses, and a multitude of specialised machines around the globe were turning out

William Timpson's factory, from the 1920s the architectural flagship of the Kettering shoe trade, went down in 1996, making way for houses. Into history too in recent years went the link with the retail stores, typified by the Market Street branch. Today in Cheshire the family is famous for its care for homeless, troubled youngsters and runs a prosperous national chain of shoe repairing and key cutting shops (George Morgan and Frank Thompson).

wrappers, paper lace and fringing, crimped cups, postcards, time recording cards, tickets, savings stamps, writing pads, food containers, cartons, boxes and machines for printing on tinfoil. There was a turnover to munitions during the war, and then such a heavy peacetime demand that orders stretched four years ahead.

By the 1950s the firm could claim "Because Timsons make rotary machines in Kettering, a Pakistani child can learn his alphabet, a New Zealander pays his bills, the Swedish government collects its taxes, the Italian licks his stamps, the Indonesian cleans his teeth, the Egyptian pays his fares, and a thousand other things work in an orderly manner." At home bus and tram tickets in a dozen cities, every Royal Mail postage stamp under 1s, *Bradshaw's Railway Guide*, and millions of wrappers were printed on Timson machines.

A great success of the 1950s was the Wun-Up press which brought newspaper production speeds to commercial printing. I saw it on test, and still remember my amazement when I glanced away, and looking back found the pile of printed leaflets had grown a yard higher in a flash.

There were many unusual jobs. One was building a printing unit for *The Times* based on two articulated lorries capable of travelling anywhere in the country and printing 12,000 eight-page copies of the paper an hour if the cold war had suddenly made it impossible for *The Times* to print in London. World wide, millions of Bibles came from Timson presses. In New York a 43-ton machine had to be hoisted to the ninth floor of a skyscraper and guided in through a window. In the 1970s the fitting shop roof had to be raised to take the biggest press to date – a 132-ton monster for printing New Zealand's telephone directories.

In recent years, running up to their centenary in 1996, Timsons concentrated on presses for printing books and forms, and they lead the world in presses for the short-run book market. Sales subsidiaries cover America and the Continent, and in 1991 with exports reaching £11m, 90% of the sales, the firm gained the Queen's Award for export achievement.

Successes of the firm, which never made a loss and never borrowed a shilling, are attributed to two factors. One is the privately owned and flexible family nature of the business, headed by three generations – Arthur Timson, Ernest Timson and son-in-law Peter Brown. The other is the value placed on the

200 employees, whose names appear in the centenary book.

Some years ago the firm was urged to move to a greenfield site, but after consulting its employees who with the works in town could walk or cycle, and go home at lunch time, it decided to stay put. Some £2m has been spent on works and offices in and around Bath Road, linked by an across-the-road bridge, and sympathetically including a fine old Primitive Methodist chapel. The heads of the firm have always been known for their closeness to the community, their friendliness and kindness, instanced by 70-year-olds who still remember their delight at being run round the block by Ernest as a young man, when he drove a scarlet Bugatti.

A red letter day was 29 April 1996 when I received an official visit from the Mayor, Councillor Mary Malin. Mary liked the Kettering books, so invited me to tea at the mayor's parlour, but twice in succession I was not able to go because of a passing illness. Jokingly complaining that I was the only man who had stood her up during her year of office, and had done it twice, she came to Beech Cottage in the mayoral limousine complete with chain of office, mayor's sergeant Ricky Hammond and the new Rector, Rev. Gordon Fisher, as escort.

Mary, a Glasgow girl, brought a delightful Scottish tea, and the visitors stayed for a couple of hours. A charming gesture, and something new for Beech Cottage which in the dim and distant past was not one of the Council's favourite buildings. See *Old Kettering and Its Defenders*.

An error I am glad to put right occurs on page 167 of Book 3. I said that Fred Barlow's initials had been removed from one of the carved shields around Rothwell Market House, so slighting his memory, but Ted Wright points out that they are still there, visible through one of the windows as you ascend the spiral stairs.

THROUGH YOUTHFUL EYES

A glimpse of High Street in the 1930s when it lived up to its name, carrying all the through A6 and local traffic in both directions, had two pick-up points for double-decker buses on the Rothwell and Desborough service, and was lined with busy shops and offices besides two cinemas, two crowded pubs and the main Council offices comes from Sybil Allen.

Then a pupil at Hawthorn Road School, Sybil was daughter of Marjorie Allen who managed the Countryside Library in High Street which she came to open in 1935 and ran for 30 years, expanding it into a bookshop:

"The latest popular fiction could be borrowed for 2d a week, a great novelty in those days. Mother told me the police were needed to control the crowd at the opening. Brought up in the country, she knew the problems and tastes of the farmers' wives who came to town once a week on market day, and she reserved books for them which she knew they would like."

High Street before the war was a close community, with everyone supportive of one another, Sybil says. In the offices above the library were the Liverpool Victoria Insurance Co. and Mr. Brodie the dentist – "the only way my mother got me in there for treatment was with the promise of a subsequent visit to the Regal, Odeon or Pavilion."

On one side of the library was the Corn Stores and on the other Ricci's Cafe which later became Dunns Outfitters. The International Stores on the corner of Gas Street (Meadow Road) was managed by Mr. Len Damon, Mr. and Mrs. Harry Fry were at Freeman, Hardy and Willis's shoe shop, and Mrs. Gardner's dress shop was opposite:

"Mother, a very sympathetic person, was entrusted with many confidences, and with so many Kettering families being inter-related her discretion was essential. She was very much missed

15

when the bookshop closed and she retired at 67. She moved from Netherfield Road to Grundy Court where she died in 1987 aged 89''.

Sybil moved to the High School, shared during the war with Dame Alice Owen School from London. Highlight of the week was a visit to the Savoy, where the Jack de Leon Company produced a different play each Monday. She left Kettering in 1948 to go to Bart's Hospital for nurse training and came back to Kettering General for three months in 1953 as staff nurse on a ward where the sister was K. Jackson, niece of matron Agnes Jackson and one of the student nurses was Pamela Harker.

Sybil made a career at Bart's becoming a ward sister and a nursing officer before retiring in 1987. She does voluntary work with the archivist at Bart's where the records date from the hospital's foundation in 1123, and finds it a privilege to have access to them. She has been admitted to the Freedom of the City of London, and among her perquisites is the right to drive her sheep across London Bridge, so long as she does it at five on a Sunday morning. And if she is found drunk and disorderly in the City the police may not arrest her, but must drive her home!

In 1954 the author was signing copies of his Northamptonshire at the behest of Mrs. Marjorie Allen at the High Street branch of Countryside Libraries. The shop sold books and ran a private lending library, one of several flourishing then, when the town had half a dozen booksellers. (Evening Telegraph).

Another youthful flashback comes from Mrs. Olive Hopson of Loughton, Essex who was an evacuee: "On 1st September 1939 war was imminent, and it was decided to evacuate our school away from London. All the children met at Walthamstow station, each with a suitcase full of clothes, a cardboard box containing a gas mask on a round-the-neck string loop and a tied-on label giving name and address. We said goodbye to our parents, and off we went in a steam train chockfull of children and teachers to an unknown destination.

"We ended up in Kettering and were taken to a school in the centre of the town, then walked in crocodile fashion along Rockingham Road, wondering what kind of life we were being pushed into. How must the people of the town have felt, having all these little cockney kids forced upon them for an unlimited period?" Olive and her friend Hilda were taken to a house they had already thought looked delightful, and were billeted with Nick and Madge Wright:

"They had two children, Patrick (then about eight – I was 12) and Neil about four. There was a live-in maid, and Mrs. Aldwinckle who came on Mondays to do washing and later in the week to do ironing. To me the house was very grand. A lovely dining room overlooking the garden where we all sat down together for meals. Silver cutlery and crystal glass. Mrs. Wright would ring a little brass bell and the maid would bring the next course. We children were never allowed to speak at table – a habit I retained long after I returned to London.

"If everything had not been so foreign to me, I think I would have enjoyed my time there. I learnt so much – how to lay a table correctly, how to polish the silver properly, and how to make meals look attractive. Though there was a war on, the Wrights lived well. They had gifts of salmon, pheasant and venison all in season, and it was there that I first tasted these things. During the shooting season the hooks inside the back door were never without game, hanging until it was ready.

"I used to help the maid with the preparation of the table for dinner parties, folding the napkins and cleaning the silver dishes. During the party Patrick and I used to sit at the top of the stairs watching through the banisters, and if there was any pudding left, we were given a taste. I remember Mrs. Wright made a delicious strawberry mousse – I had never tasted anything like it.

"I got a lot of teasing from Patrick, who on the day he acquired a snake insisted on giving me it to hold. I was terrified, but dare not show it, so I took the snake and was surprised to find that it was warm and silky soft to handle. Madge and Nick Wright eventually had four children – Patrick, Neil, Bruce and Nicholas.

"Every Sunday afternoon we would all visit Granny and Grandfather Wright at Petherton House. To me it was like a palace. The dining room was huge, and the dining table must have been able to seat at least twenty people. Mr. Wright (Nick) was one of a large family, and several of his brothers or sisters would also visit each Sunday with their own families, and all of us children sat round this enormous table for tea. We had to eat two pieces of bread and butter before we were allowed any cake or chocolate biscuits. Everything was served on silver dishes with pretty lace doilys. Granny Wright sat at the head of the table esconced behind a silver tea service with the kettle kept on the boil over a small spirit flame.

"We were allowed to play in the gardens after tea until it was time to go home. There was a long drive to the house with parking for many cars, at least six separate lawns, and one or two ponds with fish or water lilies. Some of the lawns were bordered by shrubs with lovely little wooden summer houses tucked away in the corners. How I loved visiting that garden. There was a putting green and beyond it a formal rose garden, then a hedge and behind it the kitchen garden. At the side of the house was a huge garage to take four or five cars, over which was a flat where the chauffeur lived, and a big dark room with two billiard tables in it.

"I had two Christmases with the Wrights, then early in 1941 Mrs. Wright told me she was expecting another baby, and asked if I would mind going to stay with Mrs. Aldwinckle for a few weeks, and return later if I wanted to. In fact Mrs. Aldwinckle became Aunt Betty to me and Mr. Aldwinckle Uncle Ern, and I stayed with them at 7 Leicester Street until the school returned to London. Uncle Ern worked on the railway and grew all his own vegetables on an allotment, and I have never tasted new potatoes like Uncle Ern's. They had a daughter Elsie who was about ten years older than me, but most of the time she lived with her friend Muriel and Muriel's invalid brother, so that Auntie Betty had only me to care for.

"Auntie Betty's niece Vera and her husband and daughter Anne lived at Tinwell, near Stamford, and I used to visit them on the bus and stay over a weekend. The village used to keep pigs, and the villagers would take it in turns to kill their pig, and the produce would be spread around the village so that everyone had something until the next pig was killed. I remember Vera making yards of sausages, basins full of brawn, pork pies, bacon and pigs trotters. I loved to go and help.

"Next door to Auntie Betty lived the Rigby family, and son Henry and his friend first introduced me to classical music. The friend, David Barlow, used to bring records for Henry to play on his gramophone, and I was allowed to listen. I heard the great composers, and instantly fell in love with all that wonderful music. After I left school I went to every concert I could and enjoyed many great orchestras, conductors, violinists and pianists.

"During our three years at Kettering, schooling was very difficult. First we were 'billeted' in Rockingham Road Baptist Church, which had one main hall with several rooms off it, entailing small classes and cramped working. Then we shared the Central School, and worked in shifts with them. One shift was 8.30 to 12.30, the other 1.0 to 5.0, and half days we were not in school were taken up with homework. Sports periods were on the North Park, and we used to go to Wicksteed Park and on nature rambles, but we were not allowed out in the evenings and there was a strict curfew."

Olive says she was very small and skinny for her age when she came to Kettering, even when she filled out a bit with all the good country food she was enjoying, and Patrick used to tease her. But many years later, when she came on a visit, Nick Wright said, "Well, who would have thought our little ugly duckling would turn into a swan?" She remembered Nick's compliments, for she saw him as a romantic man at heart, despite his size and bluster.

Another evacuee billeted in Rockingham Road – with the Barlows at 191 – came back in 1996 to revive memories. He is Dr. Frank (Tony) Moss, a scientist of San Francisco, who arrived in Kettering from Romford with his school in 1940. "Memories are few, but vivid," he says. "I was particularly impressed to see that Mr. Gladstone Barlow's shoes were shone every day whether he had worn them or not. I went with the family to a meet of the Pytchley, and one of the members of the household was a splendid parrot.''

Mr. Barlow would have liked Frank to join the bakery business but he went to London University and got his doctorate in chemistry, making a career in the USA with Illinois University and ICI. One of his first scientific achievements was with another lad making a 'telephone' with string and empty tins – ''It worked as long as we kept the string tight.''

Names of houses in Kettering would repay study. They show the interests or origins of people who built them, and were often called after a favourite spot. Petherton House was connected with the Toller family who came from Petherton, Devon, but a mystery is Ossian House, Rockingham Road, once the home of the shoemaking Hangers. It has gone, and John Hanger, great nephew of Henry Hanger, would like to know where it was, and why it was given that name.

Fred Moore says it stood behind the shops north of St. Andrew's Church, and he recalls the name on the gatepost. Ossian was a Celtic poet and hero with Scottish and Irish links, so someone way back must have been versed in the ballads about him.

GOODBYE ALBERT STREET

In the 1970s, when Kettering was agonising over the destruction of old Gold Street and Beech House, the residents of Albert Street were suffering even more keenly as they saw their homes disappear. Mrs. Maudie Starmer witnessed it all, and her grandson Martin Freeman recorded her recollections of Albert Street before the bulldozers came:

"Many of us were reluctant to go, and fought a long, hard battle to stay," she said, "It was heartbreaking to see those little houses torn apart." It must have been specially sad for Maudie, because her family lived in Albert Street for four generations. Her father and mother, Jack and Agnes Bates, lived at Number 27; she and her husband William Starmer lived at 43; her son-in-law and daughter Ben and Eileen Mary Freeman lived at 61, as did her grandson Martin Freeman. She stayed until near the end, leaving in 1975 after 48 years in the street. It was demolished for redevelopment as Tudor Court and Dove Court.

Maudie's father and mother moved to Albert Street in 1905, the year she was born. Jack worked for the Midland Railway as a carriage cleaner, and used to pick up odds and ends left by the passengers and put them under his cap – "there were always lots of combs and pocket knives around our house." Agnes worked in service for Mr. Eustace Lane, the solicitor in George Street, and times were hard and winters often severe. To get a grip on the icy pavements in Station Road Jack would wear 'Toe-rags' tied around his boots, and he would often bring home an old railway sleeper to be chopped up for firewood. Groups of four houses shared a well and a pump in the yard, and the families took it in turns to clean out the well – "once my father was overcome by fumes down there on a hot summer afternoon."

Her upbringing was strict. She was not allowed to read newspapers, and if she played in the garden on a Sunday her father would knock on the window and say "Don't you know what day it is?" She remembered the *Titanic* sinking, and being told by her parents that it was as long as the street, and in the 1914 war she saw a Zeppelin go over as she peeped through the curtains of the front downstairs room, where her bed had been made up for safety.

She went to the Market Place girls' school under Miss Shayler, and to the Baths for swimming lessons. "It was very dirty then, and a miserable little man held a pole and a rope under your chin and pulled you along. When they emptied the Baths we played in the water along Ford Street and Linden Avenue."

Maudie saw many old soldiers wounded or crippled in the 1914 war who did casual jobs or sold odds and ends to survive: "Many of the poor eked out a living by performing in the streets or the public houses, and if you didn't have a large family to support you there was a chance you would end up 'down the Union.' Later on when national assistance came into being things became easier for ordinary folk.

"My first recollection of vagrants, or 'tramps' as they were called, was on my frequent journeys to Woodford when I was a young girl. Mother took me to visit relatives, the nearest train station was Twywell, and we had to walk across three fields, with the only light after nightfall from Islip furnaces. We would often see tramps lying in the hedges resting as they made their way to Thrapston Union. I was very frightened, though I don't really know why. Mother used to say 'Stamp your feet hard on the ground every now and again, and they will think a man is coming along.'

"People's attitude to the tramps varied. In Albert Street they would often knock on our door. Father would usher them up the back entry as harbouring vagrants was a crime and we could have been in trouble, but we never turned them away. They rarely asked for anything more than some boiling water for their can. We normally filled it with tea and gave them bread and butter. Father made them sit and eat it, and before they left we would check that the coast was clear in the street. The rule was never to give them money as they were likely to spend it on beer. It was often said that they marked houses in some way so that other travellers knew where they would be helped, but we could not find any evidence of this."

She went to work "for two old spinsters dressmaking in The Grove. They were Miss Pickett and Miss Cundle, and I worked in the attic learning stitching, pinning and tacking at half a crown a week. They were lovely ladies, but inevitably the lure of more money made me move to the Kaycee. I was very shocked at the factory atmosphere, having been sheltered by the two spinsters. Neighbours played a large part in my youth, as did the church and its activities. We had socials and penny dances at St. Luke's rooms, and I met my future husband William Starmer there. He came from School Lane, and mother allowed us to sit and peg a rug together occasionally, always under her watchful eye. I walked home from a twopenny dance at the church rooms with him when I was 14 or 15, and when mother saw him she gave me a stern lecture. – 'If you bring any trouble home here, you'll go straight down to the Union.' Everybody feared the Union. If you went there you were beyond hope. My sister-in-law was a VAD nurse there during the first war – the place was almost like a prison. My generation never forgot the Union, and many old people were vehemently against going in as patients when it became a hospital. They associated it with past uses, whatever it was called in later years."

Maudie and Bill married at St. Luke's on New Year's Eve 1927 when the snow was piled high in the streets, and moved straight away to a little house in Freestone Row, below the Prince of Wales: "As we carried our bedding down there on our wedding night the owner of Brake's pawnshop saw us and said 'You can't bring them in now – we're closed.' He thought we wanted to pawn our belongings."

Later they moved to Maudie's childhood surroundings in Albert Street, "a very tight-knit and self-sufficient community. The shops supplied us with everything. Alf Miller ran a butcher's at the top of the street opposite the Co-op laundry, and the cattle were brought through the streets from the market in London Road to be slaughtered at the rear of the premises. Sometimes one got away from the drovers and escaped up the back entries trampling people's gardens. Bert Simms had a delightful sweet shop; milk was delivered by horse and cart, or you could fetch it yourself in a jug. George Coltman was baker and grocer. He cooked our Sunday dinners and sold cakes and confectionery. The rag and bone man kept his horse in the alleyway behind Panther's the ironmongers, which at that time was a bakehouse selling sugar, fruit and flour from large barrels. I remember the couple who owned it had an argument, and the wife who was considerably better built than her husband tripped him into the treacle barrel.

"T. W. Baileys were well known for their shoe and leather trade, and Mr. Dearlove mended shoes for the less well off. Down Thorngate Street, Mrs. Althorpe made lemonade and ginger beer, kept in pails under the stairs and sold to the locals. There was Sue Groome's paper shop, Harry Hobbs greengrocers and later fish and chip shop, Grays haberdashery and Tansleys next to the Co-op in Victoria Street. There was a funeral director's at the end

Bearing the date stone 1886 the former butcher's shop at the corner of Albert Street and Victoria Street still remains, in 1997 about to start an appropriate new career as an antique shop. Below are the flats and lawns of the new Albert Street.   (George Morgan)

of Victoria Street in a yard, and they kept a landau and hearse which was pulled by four black horses with plumes of black feathers. When anyone died they were laid out in the front parlour and friends came round to pay respects. An Irish neighbour I recall sat her husband up in his coffin and threw potatoes at him, 'to help him on his journey' she said.''

Maudie pictures some strange characters around the streets, many wounded or crippled in the 1914 war, who did what they could to survive. Others were eccentric, like one lady who prayed to the candles in Crusty Barratt's shop window. In the last war Bill went firewatching on the Co-op roof, evacuees came, Bill installed an air raid shelter in the garden and stored some wine down there, but when he brought the bottles up the mice had chewed the labels off and he could not tell which was which. Tea parties in the Co-op laundry and the United Trades Club marked the end of the war, and as the club sold drinks much cheaper than the pubs it was a popular venue for wedding teas. Everyone had an allotment, and Bill kept hens and won show certificates with his eggs. But all was not above board. Some competitors cheated by browning their eggs in tea.

Maudie's mother Agnes lived in Albert Street until her death in 1970 aged 90: ''Her house was a time capsule – no electricity or gas, no hot water, one cold tap, an open fire and a toilet at the bottom of the garden. She conceded nothing to the modern world. We took her meals down to her and locked her in at night, but things were safer then. Even in her 80s Agnes was more than a verbal match for Mr. Turner whose secondhand business in a lockup in the jetty between Albert and Alexandra Streets later became Bargain Base in Victoria Street.

''When the Council bought the street on compulsory purchase for demolition it was heartbreaking to see those little houses torn apart. I walked past Mr. Glover's, Number 59. In my childhood he had been a market gardener but became ill with chest trouble. He made flower arrangements and wreaths and hung them on large nails outside the house for selling. The rusty old nails were still there when the house fell.''

Bill, when he was a lad, used to call each Sunday at a house in Silver Street near the old Wesleyan church to take Mr. Hillyer to St. Luke's. He was a blind musician, and used to play the organ, while Bill acted as organ blower. Father Frank Wane was in charge. Bill's sister, Alice Jane Starmer, was a Sunday School teacher at the Parish Church for 50 years, and was one of those who received the Maundy money from the Queen at Peterborough Cathedral in 1975. When she was in her seventies a former pupil who had qualified as a pilot turned up and took her to Sywell for a trip over Kettering. It was her first flight, and she was thrilled, especially when he pointed out her flat in Windmill Avenue.

Martin Freeman is compiling a family tree of the Starmers, starting with 1637 parish register entries, and will be glad to hear from anyone bearing the name.

Memories of Upper Street which linked Northall and Lower Street came from Mrs. Bessie Grindrod of Leicester (née Mabbutt) who spent some of her early years at Number 8: "Our house and the adjoining houses and cottages had no back yards, gardens or rear windows, or anywhere to keep anything such as my bike, which Mr. Elks allowed me to house in his garage on Lower Street. I have happy memories of my childhood there, and of playing round the island of properties surrounded by the three streets.

The bakery at the junction of Lower Street and Upper Street which with its block went for road widening. It was a fascinating place for Madeleine Warwicker when her uncle Ernest ran it. The house was rambling, and behind it was a quadrangle with doors opening off where Ernest and his helper used to mix the dough by hand, bake in a long oven, and take the loaves to customers in a handcart. Madeleine, now Mrs. Dunmore, and her sisters Sylvia and Audrey, knew the bakery around 1930. It had become Wayman's when the picture was taken. (Ian Addis).

"At one end of Upper Street was Mr. Warwicker's cake shop and bakehouse, fronting on to Lower Street. Every Sunday morning people would take their prepared Sunday joints to be cooked, and as you can imagine the Yorkshire was very well done, a bit different from today's oven readies."

The family moved to Bayes Street in the early 1930s when the Council widened the road, taking the front room of Number 8. The triangle of properties on the south side of Upper Street has gone, and the other side has been rebuilt. But a record of the past survives in a scrap book compiled by Betty's aunt, Annie Freeman, who kept a sweet shop and cafe a few doors on the town side of the Mission House. Annie was a jolly and expansive soul, and her cafe was much frequented by the Fuller young people who played tennis on the church courts opposite, now a car park.

Annie was one of 50 confectioners listed in Beaty Hart's directory published in 1935, when Kettering had 27 public houses, four licensed hotels, six clubs, 124 general shops, 41 hairdressers including 33 ladies', 41 drapers, 38 butchers, 36 fruiterers and greengrocers, 33 tobacconists, 31 dairymen, 27 tailors, 25 bakers, 23 costumiers, 19 fried fish shops, 16 fishmongers, 18 Co-op branches, 14 florists, 13 dressmakers, 20 wireless accessory dealers, and 46 grocers.

THE RADIO BONANZA

Ninety years ago when schoolmasters kept order with the cane, Frank Wright of Bugbrooke was so different that people referred to him as 'dear old' Mr. Wright. He had a better idea than the cane for compelling attention. He was a scientist who shared his interests with his pupils, and with their help he assembled Northamptonshire's first home radio receiver. His set had an inductance seven feet long, made of a curtain pole sparsely bound with copper wire, and his variable condensers were test tubes lined with tinfoil. The youngsters were soon adept at working the tuning sliders and crystal detector, picking up time signals and news from the Eiffel Tower transmitter. There was no argument about Mr. Wright leading the field – he proudly displayed Northamptonshire's first wireless licence.

The second licence was issued to Edwin Cottingham, a Thrapston watchmaker, the third to Oundle School, and the fourth to Paul Taylor of Kettering, but their experiments were interrupted for four years. With the 1914 war approaching, the Government decided to seize all equipment that might communicate with the enemy, regardless of ownership, so that the pioneers were visited by officials who took their sets away and left polite notes of regret.

When peace returned people began to take an interest in crystal set reception, stimulated by enthusiasts like Alf Freeman who in 1923 had s set working on a Market Place stall, passing the earphones round so everyone could listen.

Home equipment was mainly crystal sets for many years. It was obvious which families had taken the plunge into the new world of ether-borne entertainment, as each set needed a high outdoor aerial, usually running from a chimney to a pole at the end of the garden. The broadcast signals, caught by the aerial were conducted down into the experimenter's room via a lead-in bored through the window frame and ending at a terminal of the crystal set, kept on a side table. The early sets looked like a 2lb jam jar made of black bakelite with the glass-enclosed crystal on top.

The listener wore headphones through which the signals flowed, returning to earth by way of another terminal fixed either to a water pipe or to a copper rod pushed down into the garden soil. They were unintelligible until the listener moved a metal 'cat's whisker' over the crystal in his detector. At certain magic spots, found by trial and error, the earphone noise would suddenly give way to clear speech, music, or a morse code transmission, and a programme could be followed and enjoyed.

A hazard was that any jarring of the table, moving the cat's whisker, would result in contact being lost, and the crystal would have to be searched again. Paul Taylor described his sufferings: "If I was lucky enough to find a good spot on the crystal, and keep the cat's whisker steady, I could get the Eiffel Tower, Pondhu, and the big German station at Hauen. If I lost the spot on the crystal, I had to go down into the yard and start the car engine, then go back up and juggle about with the cat's whisker and crystal until I could hear the car ignition sparks in the headphones, run down again, turn off the engine, and run up once more to return to the set. If in the meantime someone knocked the table, it meant starting all over again." (Paul tuned to his car engine sparks because their crackle would have sounded much louder than the distant radio station, and would have yielded a good spot on the crystal more quickly.)

Paul's licence, though fourth in the County, was the first in Kettering when it was issued in 1912. His ambition was to establish a transmitter, and a Leicester firm had made equipment to his design, but he abandoned this when his devices were 'interned.' After the war, wireless was at first merely a timekeeping aide. Watch and clock repairers needed to know the correct time, and they depended on time signals broadcast on the Continent. George Horden, for example, maintained Kettering parish church clock, and had the responsibility of firing the maroon at exactly eleven o'clock on Armistice Day for the Two Minutes Silence. He had his own wireless, carried in a foot-square wooden case, purpose-built to pick up the exact time from transmitters in Berlin and Paris. They sent out time signals and

OUR FIRST WIRELESS AERIAL.

EVENING TELEGRAPH

From an old cutting, this historic photograph shows one of Kettering's first wireless aerials being erected in September 1922 at the Evening Telegraph offices in Dryland Street. It picked up time signals from the Continent and the first concerts broadcast by Marconi from Chelmsford. Clock repairers called in to set their timepieces, and townspeople to 'listen in'. The British Broadcasting Company (later BBC) had just been formed by radio manufacturers. The aerial was so high that the Fire Brigade under Captain Riddle had to fix it. (Wilf Elmore).

dots a second apart which could be used to set clock pendulums. The *Evening Telegraph* used wireless to obtain the correct time, and watch and clock repairers without sets used to call at the office to check their master watches.

By 1922 the first experimental broadcasts of speech and music by Marconi engineers at Writtle, Chelmsford were received every Tuesday evening at the *Telegraph* office, and prominent townspeople paid visits to hear this remarkable novelty. Councillor Deeley went on to a committee meeting where he told fellow members he had been listening to a concert at Chelmsford, and was promptly informed that he must be trifling with the truth. The Prince of Wales broadcast to Scouts from Marconi House, and Kettering members gathered at the newspaper office to hear him.

The great step forward in home radio came in 1925 when Daventry 5XX was opened, potentially able to reach thousands of crystal sets and a growing number of valve sets within 100 miles radius. For the station opening the British Broadcasting Company, as it then was, laid on a long-distance reception for the Postmaster General and chief guests, welcoming them at Euston Station and shepherding them by rail to Daventry and the new buildings below the aerials on Borough Hill.

The first words on air fell to Mr. John Reith, who as managing director announced ''Daventry calling . . .'' and went on to describe the new station and the role it would play. He had to stand on a marked spot on the carpet to address, three feet away, a microphone described as 'looking like a segment of cheese on a bureau.' It emerged that Kettering had been considered as a site for the transmitter, but Daventry stood higher above sea level.

National transmitters gave a compulsive urge to the growth of home radio, and soon it was rare to find a back garden without a wireless mast. Philip Hague remembers: ''Looking up Kingsley Avenue, one saw a forest of poles in the back gardens. From the top of each pole an aerial stretched to a chimney on the house. A down wire led through a window frame to the set, and the earth spike driven into the soil of the garden had to be kept damp to ensure good reception.

''The nearest BBC stations were Daventry and Droitwich. Tuning meant manipulating cat's whisker and crystal, and coils and condensers improved the signal, which some people amplified by placing the earphones in a tin basin. Loudspeaker sets came in about 1925 and were in use by the 1930s, their brightly-glowing valves residing in walnut cabinets. These sets used a high voltage dry battery and a low voltage accumulator which had to be taken once a week to an electrical shop for recharging. People had two accumulators, one in use and the other away on charge. Taking one's accumulator in its wire holder to the shop became a ritual, almost like walking the dog. Through the 'thirties battery sets were gradually replaced by mains 'superheterodynes', some with magic eye tuning and claiming to receive America.'' One of the first valve sets, a Tangent, was advertised as a BBC set with four valves, a HT Battery, a six volt 100 amp hour accumulator and a pair of 1,000 ohm loudspeakers, price £40 including all royalties and BBC fees. It was a no-nonsense black bakelite box with tuning knobs.

These developments released an enormous bonanza for the radio industry, financing new stores and businesses in shopping streets everywhere. Kettering in the mid-thirties had 20 radio and accessory firms which grew from small beginnings, providing mass-produced parts for do-it-yourself crystal sets which many people bought, but they found it was no easy job to install a set. Fitting the do-it-yourself pieces together was simple, but erecting the aerial was a man's job, entailing putting ladders up to the chimney to fix one end, and concreting in a 30-foot pole at the bottom of the garden to support the other. Most people had the whole job done by professionals, which brought into the picture two men who became lifelong leading figures in the Kettering radio trade.

Paul Taylor and Arthur York both sprang from cycle and motor trade families. Paul was the son of Harry Taylor, whose shop on the Montagu-Silver Street corner supplied a generation with their Humber bikes. Arthur's father Herbert was a foreman at Ball's foundry, Rothwell, built a gas engine, started his workshop at the back of 10 Edgell Street and began to sell bikes and cars, also serving as works engineer at Loake Brothers, shoe manufacturers.

H. York and Sons developed in two sections, Ray handling the garage and car sales, and Arthur the cycle trade. Ray died in middle life, and that side of the business closed, but Arthur extended the cycles side to take in wireless. Through the car trade they met Wally Jacques of Thrapston who knew about do-it-yourself crystal sets, and Arthur and his father rigged the gas engine to cut up hundreds of ebonite panels into ready-made parts for sale. The enterprise flourished up to 1929-30 when commercial all-mains sets appeared. ''From 1924 the demand was enormous,'' Arthur recalled.

Meanwhile Paul Taylor forged ahead, pioneering the sale of sets. His first customer was Herbert Daniels, for 35 years manager and secretary of the Kaycee clothing factory, which he made into one of the town's biggest employers. Herbert held many public offices, but when he reached his 100th birthday and was asked for some interesting point about himself, he proudly laid claim to the ownership of Kettering's first wireless, after Paul Taylor.

Paul and Arthur, as friendly rivals, clocked up lots of 'firsts'. In 1923 Paul fitted a Burndept Etherphone into Bagshaws' coach 'Phyllis' – the town's first mobile radio. In 1925 he was first with public address amplifiers for large gatherings. The same year he persuaded owners of Burndept sets to provide wireless for the General Hospital, a scheme copied by London hospitals. In 1928 he demonstrated in his Silver Street window the first printed pictures received by radio. When Baird 30-line TV opened he claimed the first reception in the town. In 1933 he established Radiomains, Kettering's first cable radio system, and in 1935 was first in the country to pioneer all-in maintenance. He made successful Marconiphone TV tests in 1938 at Kettering Radio Exhibition, opened by Ann Zeigler.

Meanwhile Arthur's York and Sons opened on Bakehouse Hill with the coming of all-mains radio, and when Munn and Felton's

In the radio era which began with crystal sets in the early 1920s, friendly retail rivals were Paul Taylor (left) and Arthur York. They delighted in scoring ''firsts'' over one another as new developments came along.
(Peter Taylor & Susan Glover).

Band broadcast for the first time in 1934 he lent out radio sets free. Four dozen went out, and sales were so good that only five came back. Yorks gave Kettering's first 405-line TV demonstration in 1937, pictures brought in by aerial on top of a 40-rung ladder at Mr. Dainty's Poplars Farm – the highest ground. Yorks were first to offer a local TV rental scheme in 1954, followed by a TV relay system, and in 1957 they owned the first fleet of radio controlled vans.

Arthur eventually acquired control of Paul Taylor and Partners, and became managing director of half a dozen east midland radio and TV retail and maintenance firms. He obtained an early experimental 405-line colour set from the Murphy laboratories and donated it to Kettering Museum. An important feature is that the set has quickly removable panels at the sides and top which enabled the design team to reach any part of the circuitry quickly to put new ideas into practice. There were only two of the sets. One was given to the House of Commons for demonstration to MPs, but was burnt out when it was left switched on with the protective cover in place. This means that the Kettering set is unique, said Arthur, unless there is something similar at South Kensington.

Who were the first Kettering broadcasters? This is a tricky one to answer, and I expect half a dozen readers will be putting pen to paper to offer names. From the *Evening Telegraph* files it seems that Haydn Sail was the first, with piano solos from Nottingham as early as August 1925. He gave freqent organ recitals from Southwark Cathedral, and piano recitals and baritone solos from Birmingham. He conducted Kettering Ladies Choir and Kettering Choral Society in several broadcasts, and gave organ recitals from Fuller.

Other early broadcasters were Maud Loake, Constance Sharman, Arthur Trayhurn, Frank Southwell and Horace Lansberry (singers), Mrs. Ralph Wicksteed (cello) and 40 boys and girls who in 1927 took part in St. Mary's School Nativity play, broadcast from the school buildings. In 1930 the Rev. Greville Cooke arranged services from Cransley parish church.

Lester Mudditt was a regular voice on the air in the 1930s, figuring regularly in drama, feature and musical comedy programmes, and particularly well known for his part in the Paul Temple series. Also in the 'thirties Ron Tingle played the musical saw, Howard Lee the piano, the Tennyson Quartet broadcast from Birmingham, and the Co-op Male Voice Choir were on the air conducted by Charles Adams and accompanied by William McKenna.

From 1937 the Kettering String Trio (Janet and Joyce Maddison and Hope Timpson) figured regularly, and in 1947 Janet and Dr. Ken Barritt, formerly of Walgrave, pianist and organist, combined in playing his Sonata in B Major. Mr. and Mrs. Ray Sadler broadcast songs at the piano, Lester Mudditt and Courtney Hope of Wellingborough were in the Midland Five O'Clock Follies, Bertha Wilmott, hostess of Spinney Hill Hotel was a famous pop singer, and specialised talks came from Robert Bernard of Kettering Grammar School (a poultry fancier), and Ron Burton of Broughton (the rook census). Boot and shoe trade broadcasters included the Versatile Trio and Odette Punch.

The Central Hall was for a generation the home of leading operatic and dramatic societies, the eisteddfod, shows of ballet schools, and of Saturday night dances for which the seats were removed and where many a romance began. The hall hosted important meetings and social events, and at times national conferences. It was a cradle of broadcasters. Architect R. J. Williams designed the building, which is remembered with universal affection. (KICS)

Sixteen-year-old Nona Blamire was regularly on the air from 1946, when in a serial 'We Couldn't Leave Dinah' she took the parts of a German child and a French child while still at the Ursuline Convent School, specialising in languages.

In the 1930s the BBC had live 'Listeners Answer Back' sessions, and Dennis Morris came to Kettering to broadcast listeners' views. There were so many questions that they went on long after the broadcast had finished: Why no early morning programmes? – Because of the cost; Why are jokes about drink not censored? – They are if necessary; Why are symphony concerts allowed to finish while variety is faded out? – Fading out a great artistic work would be undesirable; Organ recitals are short and scrappy, and we want more plays on Sunday; Why can't we have more Gilbert and Sullivan? – Reasons of copyright; Why are crooners encouraged? – Some people find them most enjoyable; Why always play light music at midday? – Bach doesn't go with beefsteak and kidney pud. Today the questions would be rather less reverent!

White haired William Martin, retired chief reporter of the *Evening Telegraph* showed vision of the future when he said that then, in 1939, broadcasts had largely superseded political meetings. He felt that assistance should be given to leaders of national organisations to broadcast their views.

The names of the questioners were not broadcast and local listeners had an interesting time trying to identify them. The *Telegraph* thoughtfully gave their names, among them Wilf Elmore, Mrs. Keith Coles, William Grinham, Frank Summerley, Pat Wills, George Howard, Frank Thompson and Joan Coles. Dennis promised that soon TV would be within financial reach of everyone, and the screen would not be small and difficult to look at.

If he is still around, he must be astonished at the way his promise had been more than fulfilled 60 years later, with skydish aerials communing with satellites and setting a trend like the back garden masts of the 1920s.

A CHURCH – ST. MARY'S

"Don't forget," said David Newton, "you still have to do the churches." His words brought me face to face with a job I'd been dodging because of its size. Kettering, nicknamed 'the Holy City' in the 1930s, when it had some thirty places of worship, is in many ways the product of its churches, spiritually and materially. The most obvious sign is the twin commercial centres, based on Market Place and Gold Street. They exist because in times past the Churchpeople gathered round the Parish Church, while the Free Church families lived close to Toller and Fuller, and each community developed its own shops and businesses. David, a Wellingborough minister's son, remembers this from his time at the *Evening Telegraph* en route to editing the venerable *Stamford Mercury*.

So, where to begin, bearing in mind that each church may need a chapter? Through the years I've maintained files on the churches, so I picked the bulkiest – St. Mary's – in which my notes were supplemented by warm-hearted flashbacks from the Rev. G. R. J. Round (vicar of All Saints) and parishioners Geoff Bellamy, Fred Blount, Jim Dodge, Effie Panther, Jack Payne and Dorothy Woollard, and from it came this chapter.

A Church of England district, then a parish for over a century, and with 9,000 living in it, St. Mary's has been fascinating from the word go. The stone-built church was a magnificent gift to Kettering from a benefactress who died without being able to view it, and through the years its parishioners have striven to emulate her generosity.

They set themselves to achieve beauty in worship, making a distinctive devotional appeal through decor, colour, pre-Reformation services, statues and symbols, music and prayer. St. Mary's is High Church, once a source of division, but no longer so. Ecumenically, it lies among streets named after Nonconformist heroes Fuller, Toller, Knibb and Carey, while a fifth – Bridge Street – is a reminder of metaphorical bridges to Christian unity.

St. Mary's owes its existence to Lady Elizabeth Villiers, widow of Lt. Col. Frederick Villiers, Coldstream Guards, who lived at Sulby Hall on the Warwickshire border. There was no church at Sulby, and Lady Elizabeth worshipped at neighbouring Sibbertoft, where she re-roofed an aisle of St. Helen's church and in 1872 donated the clock in memory of her husband. She became a great friend of the curate, Rev. Henry Lindsay, and after he was appointed Rector of Kettering Lady Elizabeth took a great interest in the town, known to her as her uncle William Hope lived at Rushton Hall and served as County Sheriff.

Kettering, at the time of its Victorian expansion, had great need for new churches, and hearing of the problem from Canon Lindsay Elizabeth undertook to provide one entirely at her own expense, expressing three wishes. Her church must not be on a main road, it must stand among the homes of the town's poorest inhabitants, and her bounty must remain anonymous.

Elizabeth was by birth Lady Elizabeth de Reede de Ginkell, daughter of the 8th Earl of Athlone, and her marriage to Col. Villiers joined families prominent in the troubled times of William and Mary. Her ancestor Godert de Ginkell, came over with William of Orange in 1688, commanded William's army in the Irish campaign of 1691, was made Earl of Athlone and served as second in command to the Duke of Marlborough in the war with France.

Frederick's ancestor, Edward Villiers, had a more modest start as master of the horse to Mary, but went as envoy to Holland and Paris, served as secretary of state 1700-01, and became the first Earl of Jersey. His sister became notorious, going to Holland as matron-of-honour to Mary, and becoming the mistress of William, meddling in affairs of state. He cast her off in 1694, the year Mary died, and she married the Earl of Orkney. Frederick's father, the 5th Earl, held Court offices and in 1804 married the prospective heiress of banker Robert Child, assuming Child as an additional name.

In accordance with Lady Elizabeth's wishes, St. Mary's stands away from Stamford Road, and was originally among tiny crowded houses well described by Dorothy Woollard: "Switch

40

*Ironstone Gothic St. Mary's, built
1893-5, was given to Kettering by
a wealthy benefactress who died
before she could see it completed.
She asked for the church to be
built among what were then some
of the poorest streets. A lofty
campanile (right) was planned as
a memorial to Fr. Glaister but the
cost proved too great.
(Gotch, Saunders and Surridge).*

on your TV and watch the opening scene of Coronation Street.
That is what Knibb Stret was like, but those houses have all been
demolished. When demolition was going on a workman called

41

me over. 'Look at these foundations,' he said, 'They would have lasted for ever.' ''

Allan Page, attending church in the 1930s, saw Knibb Street children running about shoeless. Jim Dodge recalls: ''St. Mary's is late Victorian built in heavy ironstone with a steeply pitched tiled roof and a small bell tower over the vestry. A badly surfaced lane on the north side ran by the church railings, from the slaughterhouse at the top to a one-storey leather factory at the bottom. A small sloping lawn provided the only place for wedding photographs, green and empty between the long undivided clumps of blue flags. The exterior of the church shared the drab and muted tones of the terraces and factories, and the walls were streaked here and there with dark green damp. Nothing suggested the almost Byzantine colour of the interior, concealed like a moth in a chrysalis.''

Lady Elizabeth died in 1897 aged 76, two years after the church was finished, and her name was kept secret for 25 years until revealed by the Rev. Alex Lindsay, one of Canon Lindsay's sons. Preaching the silver jubilee sermon, he said that at last he felt able to disclose the identity of their generous-hearted patron.

To obtain some idea of her munificence in today's money we can add two noughts at least to the pre-1914 total of £7,000. Hensons of Wellingborough were the contractors, and the architect was J. A. Gotch, whose design exhibited at the Royal Academy included a splendid campanile, never built because of the great additional expense.

Fr. Round, publishing a golden jubilee history in 1945, looked back on lively times before Elizabeth's church appeared. The first St. Mary's was a temporary tin building brought from Philbeach Gardens, South Kensington, where it had been St. Cuthbert's in charge of Canon Bliss. He was brother-in-law to Canon Lindsay, and readily handed it to Kettering when a permanent St. Cuthbert's was built.

Curate-in-charge Rev. Frederick Deane noted: ''In those days St. Mary's district was wild and rough, and at first my evening sermons were punctuated by bricks and big stones falling on the roof. Bradlaugh's influence was strong, and the Church was regarded as a citadel of Toryism, but I was a supporter of the Labour Party and a Christian socialist, and in any case everyone respected Canon Lindsay – Canon Street and Lindsay Street are named in honour of him. He tramped round Kettering visiting every sick person, which enabled me to soften opposition to the Church. Edmund Street was the limit of town extension, the boot work was done in backyard workshops, and a curate could sit and talk with the men at any hour.''

Frederick, later on Bishop of Aberdeen and the Orkneys, was so successful that more children attended his catechism class than the church could hold. He married Caroline Lindsay, one of the Canon's four sons and nine daughters, but this did not please Canon Bernard Wilson who succeeded her father as rector and as a High Churchman preferred single clergy. After the marriage he issued an ultimatum to his curates stating ''Any member of the staff becoming engaged to be married must forthwith resign.'' Imagine that today!

The man who more than anyone set his seal on St. Mary's was the Rev. Francis Harvey Glaister. A Cambridge MA, he was ordained deacon in 1904 at Rochester Cathedral after London University and Lincoln Theological College. He served as curate at All Saints, Rotherhithe, was ordained priest and spent four years at St. Peter's, Vauxhall, before coming to St. Mary's as curate in charge in 1911. He was the first vicar when in 1916 St. Mary's became a parish, and continued until 1930 when he died, after a long illness, in hospital at Leicester.

He was broad shouldered, vigorous and in his prime when he took over, which was just as well since as a High Churchman he did not have an easy path to follow. The Oxford Movement, started a century before by John Keble and John Henry (later Cardinal) Newman, among others, had come to fruition in the Church of England. Its followers looked back to the pre-Reformation Catholic roots of the Church rather than to its Protestant origins, and their worship was close to the Roman ritual.

Consequently St. Mary's history was that of a local Catholic revival. As Fr. Round rcords, sung Mass was restored, daily Mass began, full vestments were worn, candles and incense were used, and midnight Mass at Christmas and the reservation of the Sacrament became normal.

Jim Dodge, an altar boy, remembers ''at midnight Mass on Christmas Eve we had to kneel for up to an hour as the communicants moved slowly in two long lines to the altar rails.

On Wednesdays in Lent I used to hurry along from school for Stations of the Cross. The tiles of the chancel chilled my feet as we served barefoot on Good Friday. One of the most remarkable things about St. Mary's was its location. It had no social standing whatever – truly Christian in a way.''

It was Fr. Glaister's pride and joy to beautify his beloved St. Mary's. As he walked round Kettering his ever-watchful eye noticed treasures that would add to the appeal of the church. At Mr. C. W. Ward's he found the great tryptich picture of the Last Supper which ornaments the north chancel wall. By royal academician Thomas Luny (1759-1837) it had been in Lord Wantage's collection at Overstone, and Mr. Ward contributed half the cost.

At stonemason W. T. Cox's Fr. Glaister noticed in embryo a side altar of alabaster designed by Sir Thomas Jackson and sculptured by Sir Hamo Thornycroft. Mrs. Phyllis Purdy of Northampton recalls that it was originally a great fireplace in Rushton Hall. It was adapted as the congregation's beautiful memorial to their 1914-18 war dead. The spectacular rood beam was given anonymously in memory of Miss Isabella Maltby who did much practical work to add to the church. Other additions were the west window designed by Martin Travers and the first Stations of the Cross after designs by Noyes Lewis. As the church increased in beauty it attracted vandals, and a precaution forced upon the congregation was the installation of massive interior ornamental railings and gates, to close off the body of the church from the entrance.

During the first war Fr. Glaister served as a chaplain in France, and was chosen to go to St. James's Palace to receive his Victory and Overseas medals from the Prince of Wales, later Edward VIII. He was a forceful preacher, and once a month instead of a sermon he answered questions from the pulpit. His death, the end of an era, came after an operation for ear trouble which he lacked the strength to withstand.

In a study of St. Mary's between 1920 and 1938 Jack Payne hits off the spirit of the times: ''During the early 1920s, Sunday was a special day for everyone, whether religious or not. Most people attended church, chapel, or some religious meeting. We, living in the east end of Kettering, were taken to St. Mary's as babes in arms until we could walk, then we went with brothers and sisters like many other families.

"I joined the choir when I was six or seven. In six months probation Sidney Loasby – nicknamed Koff – sorted you out. An expert organist and teacher, in gown and mortarboard, he ruled us with a firm but tender hand. Choir practice was Wednesday night for boys and Friday night for men, and the music was Plainsong, Byrd, Gibbons, Tallis and Bach. The Asperges, Kyrie, Gloria and Creed with the introits and anthems sung by the cantors were all different as we moved through the Church's year.

"We were taught to read music from a blackboard in the vestry, then we went into the chancel. All would be quiet, and Koff would play each part separately. Then it was a deep breath, all standing up straight, a chord from the organ, and as we sang we could see his eyes in the mirror above, watching each one of us. Sadly, Koff was to leave us about 1930 to go as organist at SS Peter and Paul. All the well-known families sang in the choir, and by the example they gave us boys you could see they were singing to the glory of God."

Jack became an altar server, learning the Mass sequence from the Preparation to the Last Gospel: "Everything had to be done quietly and with reverence, and to this end there were rules which were always obeyed. All servers wore a cassock when in the sanctuary, and slippers which were kept in pigeonholes in the choir vestry. Cyril Hircock, sacristan for many years, guided us into the correct ways, laying out the vestments in the form of the letters IHS.

"For Evensong in those days there were no servers, just the choir and the vicar taking the service from his stall, George Hanger reading the lessons, and then the vicar giving his sermon, walking up and down the centre aisle and quietly talking to the congregation. There were very few empty seats. After the sermon he would kneel at the back of the church in the centre aisle for the intercessions, lasting about 15 minutes, then the last hymn, perhaps 'The day Thou gavest, Lord, is ended', during which he would walk slowly to the altar to give the final blessing."

Going to church with his mother was an unforgettable experience for Jim Dodge: "Mum's confidence was quiet and unassailable, like her faith, and possibly a product of it. She did not need to assert her faith, it simply shone through her. She possessed it and spoke of it in the natural course of things, and it was indelibly her. In St. Mary's there was a statue of the Virgin, blue robed and white veiled, small and with downcast eyes. If I stood by Mum at Evensong as she recited the Magnificat she became the Virgin herself, and glowed with the lowliness of His handmaiden.

> 'He hath scattered the proud in the imagination of their hearts.
> He hath put down the mighty from their seats and hath
>   exalted the humble and meek.
> He hath filled the hungry with good things, and the rich he
>   hath sent empty away . . .'

She spoke the words clearly but quietly, partly to the statue, partly to herself, and as they did at Communion the crowsfeet at the corners of her eyes relaxed, and she smiled slightly. I was even then half aware of her separateness, of an almost physical withdrawal that was at the root of her strength. It wasn't necessary for her to be let depart in peace. She was all coolness and calm when she dipped her finger in holy water to sign the cross on her forehead as we left."

Jack Payne found ample opportunity for all age groups at St. Mary's. Sunday School treats were to the Wicksteed Park, the children sitting on bales of straw on horsedrawn railway drays. Prizes for the sports came from Doris Joyce who kept a shop in Thorngate Street. In later years the children met at the school, mugs in hand and tickets pinned to lapels, to march behind Fuller Mission Band down Stamford Road, Gold Street and High Street to the station, whence a special train took them to Rushton. Again behind the band they marched to a farmer's field for sports and games. Tea prepared by the mothers came from two ex-WD urns, and the goodies included party cakes made in 2'6" × 18" trays by Barlows. Then, all tired, back to the station and home.

Other red letter days were Kettering Feast and Rogation Sundays. For the feast service at SS Peter and Paul, St. Mary's went in procession, joining up with All Saints at the top of Gold Street. Jack remembers that at rogationtide there would be a procession from St. Mary's after Evensong up Clarence Road to Avondale Road, stopping to bless the allotments where the Laburnum estate is now, then down Avondale Road to the allotments in Weekley Road, then to Windmill Avenue allotments, and back to the church, Cyril Hircock leading with crucifix, holy water and incense. Prayers were for a blessing on the crops and on the places of employment.

Fr. Round lists an amazing array of parish organisations including the missionary guild, company of service, mothers union, evening working party, church help society, the church union branch, guild of all souls, Sunday schools, church council, scouts, cubs, guides and brownies, operatic society and religious drama group.

Effie Panther remembers the lives of all the families revolving round the church and its activities, branching out into socials where young people learnt to dance, and unofficial shorthand classes in the vestry: "The guides and brownies were run by Jessie and Connie Clarke who were always in church on Sunday. The church owned an old house in Lawson Street with an unkempt and derelict garden which ran down to the swimming baths, and the scouts, guides and brownies used it. There was no heating, and Connie used to bring a basket with a few sticks and bits of coal in it so that we could have a glimmer of a fire. It was all dark and eerie at the top of the garden, and there were plenty of 'ghosts', but our parents never felt any need to be concerned about us in those days."

A great deal of practical work was done by the evening working party, called by Fr. Glaister "The old firm that never lets me down." The workers looked after and renewed practically everything in the church – they made all the altar linen and frontals, paid for or made most of the vestments, and did redecoration including such difficult jobs as the rood beam and the altar canopy.

Fred Blount entered a very active social whirl based on the school in Fuller Street. Cecil Ashby's band – he was in the choir – played for socials. Miss Howard organised the Sunday schools, and the operatic society for people of 15 upwards was run by its conductor Miss Neal, sister of Mr. J. C. Neal the Station Road builder, later manager of the Wicksteed Park. Mr. Skews assisted in this important project which went on for 20 years each annual production raising cash for church funds, buying the music and libretto for the next show, and going on tour round other parishes. The religious drama group was formed by schoolmaster William Simms.

Effie can picture many of the faithful: "The Warren family girls occupied a whole row at Evensong. Mr. Warren and his sons were leaders of the choir with Bert Abbott, Frank Billings and others. Servers were Cyril Hircock, Obed Bye, Jack, Harold and Bill Payne. Tax official Bill Barber was a churchwarden, and his wife, a hard worker for socials and whist drives, was deaf. Mrs. Shepherdson prayed every day that her hearing would be restored, and such is the power of prayer that it did happen some years later. Blanche Ashby was another lovely person. Her husband Cecil, such a good pianist, fell from a ladder and broke his leg so badly that after two years or more in and out of hospital he had to lose it. He was never quite well after that, and died too soon.

"Miss Goode, who lived next to the factory in Rutland Street, used to superintend the older Sunday School, and was another regular. She taught the piano, and her brother Ted was mayor. George Hanger, the lay reader, was most important. He was small and bald with gold rimmed glasses, and you could hear his sonorous voice loud and clear all over the church when he read the lessons.

"Mr. A. J. Shepherdson churchwarden, lay reader and headmaster of the senior mixed school, and his wife sat on the right in church. He was a tall, imposing presence, always to be seen round the parish, walking to or from school or church, which had a beneficial effect on all the youth of the area. He and his wife were wonderful people, involved in all aspects of the community, and the church was Mrs. Shepherdson's life.

"She heard that my father had never had a grapefruit – they were not common in the shops in those days – so one evening she knocked at the door with her basket containing a grapefruit, which she proceeded to cut up with her little silver knife. She even brought a cherry to garnish it. They lived at 3, Naseby Road, which they had built among the people they served, and when Shep died it was bequeathed to the church for the use of a curate. They were godparents to lots of children of parishioners and always remembered birthdays.

Jack Payne remembers Shep's later years: "He retired in 1938 and lost his wife. We could see him going downhill, and when the war came it was his saviour. He joined the Home Guard, had been an infantry captain in the first war, and was

48

Two priests fondly remembered at St. Mary's are Rev. Francis Glaister (right) and Rev. Hubert Rokeby. Fr. Glaister, the first vicar, worked tirelessly to enrich the services and beautify the church. Fr. Rokeby, from fortunate circumstances, generously passed round the silver spoon. (Fred Blount).

promoted to major. It gave him a new lease of life.''

As Jack looks back, scores of faces pass before him. People in the choir were Arthur and Fred Clipstone, Len Palmer, Fred Blount, Walter Pamplin, Stan and Melbourne Tassell, Bill Newbold, Colin Garbett, John Newbold, Jack Clark, Will Stanger, Ray Knight, Cliff Wilcox and George Abbott.

The Bible class was run by Ted Goode, cricketer, church-warden, councillor and mayor, and Luke Garbett; the 8th Scouts by Tom Baxter, Obed Bye and Ray Knight; the Sunday schools by George Hanger, Will Stanger, Lilian Tansley and Doris Joyce; Harry Bridgeman did many jobs as caretaker, and John Wallin walked twice from Lower Street every Sunday to act as thurifer. One bitterly cold day he turned up in his wife's fur coat. There were Elsie Blackwell, Arthur Crask who never missed a Sunday though disabled in the war, Miss Yeates the shrewd Scottish housekeeper for Fr. Glaister, Bernard Knight of the choir and scouts, and an organist, Mr. Aveling the verger, with sons Jim, Bob and Ralph, all servers, and daughters Joan and Phyllis.

Mr. and Mrs. Warren came with son Bill and sisters Kath, Joan and Betty, Tom Griggs was a churchwarden and Mill Road tailor, Jack and Philip Griggs were servers, Herbert Hayes was one of the servers longest in office, Lorna his wife was in charge of the sewing party for years, Elsie and Joan were Sunday School teachers, Miss Brunsden a school teacher with missionary work a great interest, and others were Miss Cruikshank infants headmistress, Mr. and Mrs. Sturman and Nora, Frank and Mrs. Underwood, Mr. and Mrs. Abbott and Reg, server and parochial church council secretary, with George, choirman and councillor, Kath and Hilda, daughters of Esther Clark of Edmund Street who took the children for walks, and Eric Hodson organist.

The Rev. Hubert Denys Eddowes Rokeby, assistant priest from 1928 to 1932, was one of those delightful people who, having a private income, did not live selfishly but passed round the silver spoon. His father, Samuel, was in the Indian Civil Service and claimed to have begun the first modern sewerage system in Bombay. His mother, Lucy Boult, was from the Liverpool trading family that produced conductor Sir Adrian. His father died in middle age, and Denys and his mother returned to England so that he could go to Cambridge where he read maths and economics. Choosing the Church for his life's work, he wished to serve in the Peterborough diocese, and the Bishop had the happy idea that he should be ordained deacon at St. Mary's, for which he was destined. The church was packed, and extra seating had to be brought in.

There are two stories about his pay from St. Mary's. One is that he gave his services free, and the other from Fr. Round is that he took only half pay. He had a likeable down-to-earth manner and never wanted it to be known that he was well-to-do, but this showed in his lifestyle as he lived in an attractive house in London Road almost opposite The Grove and employed a gardener, housekeeper, valet and maid. He had a private grass tennis court behind Cheney's nursery in Windmill Avenue which he threw open to the church young people, and he played cricket with their team.

Jack Payne remembers: "One Sunday he climbed into the pulpit with two lovely black eyes, and had to explain 'Fred Blount sent down a fast one. I got in the way.' On Whit Monday we cycled to Burghley House and played a cricket XI fielded by Lord Burghley, the famous Olympic hurdler, who played. We lost, but we put up a good show . . ." Before the 20-mile cycle ride and the match, Jack had been up with the lark and done his paper round. Oh, the boundless energy of youth.

Fr. Rokeby, in organising the younger element, sometimes had to administer rough justice. He arranged lots of outings to Oxford,

Cambridge, Whipsnade, the Zoo and Stratford, to name a few, and on a trip to London Jack recalls that somebody in the compartment snatched Colin Garbett's grammar school cap. It was thrown merrily around, with him trying to recover it, and not unexpectedly it went out of the window. "Fr. Rokeby ruled that all boys in the compartment must buy Colin a new cap, and we had to pay sixpence each. For the next few weeks we all used to shout 'Be careful with our cap, Colin.' The KGS caps and badges had to be bought from Miss Jenkinson's in High Street, and the High School equipment was available only from Miss Thomas's baby linen shop near Post Office Arcade according to Grace Thornton, who adds: "An example of unfair male preferences even then was that the girls had to pay 2d extra for their badges on top of the boys 6d."

Jack goes on: "Fr. Rokeby formed a guild for teenagers dedicated to a boy martyr. Meetings were held in the choir vestry, and by his example, kindness and patience he taught us a lot about life during those formative years. After Evensong on Sunday nights a group of us would walk up to his house for a game of cards etc., and always left at nine o'clock." The choirmen would go to the vicar's house on the roundabout in Stamford Road, which Effie Panther remembers had been the home of W. B. Gash, art master at Kettering Grammar School whose pretty daughter Margaret was a talented pupil of her father.

Fred Blount contributes more about Fr. Rokeby: 'He was one of the most sincere men I have ever met. At the time I am thinking of he lived with his mother at 73, London Road, welcoming people to parties, and entertaining visitors from away, including the Rev. Douglas Cooper who became Fr. Glaister's successor. One Sunday after Evensong he very unwisely let us loose in his orchard. I think he must have had a bit of trouble with his chauffeur-gardener as a result, because after that we were only given five minutes in which to help ourselves before leaving at 9 pm. The orchard had apricots and peaches along the walls, pears, all sorts of apples, and on the side of the garage was a trained cherry with large red fruit. We tried them, but slipped up because they were morellos, as bitter as vinegar.

"When we in our choir group were about 13 years old we seriously blotted our copybooks. A group of seven-year-olds from the school joined the choir, but they could not sing much and some could not even read. On our quarterly pay day we received the usual 1s 6d, but to our astonishment the new juniors got 2d more. We put our heads together and went on strike, sitting in the back row of the church at Evensong instead of in the choir. For this, some of the elders wanted us sacked from the choir, and there was even talk of excommunication.

"The outcome was that my mother asked Fr. Rokeby to come to see her, and she pointed out that if we were turned out of the choir it was unlikely that we would ever come to church again. He understood, straightened things out, and we were all reinstated.

"Fr. Rokeby's hobby was collecting picture postcards covering towns, villages and churches, and railway lines, engines and stations. He had so many that they were housed in wall-to-wall sets of shelves. He taught us to play bridge, pontoon, and other card games, and was keenly interested in all the youth groups. He drove an open Swift car which was always available for transport, and when the scouts went to camp he had a bell tent to himself. He enjoyed and almost invited practical jokes, and one morning was pinned to the ground inside his tent when by arrangement we all got up early and released his guy ropes simultaneously."

Fred's age group included Ralph Kelly, Bernard Driver, Harold Steff, Leslie, Alan and Philip Kirk (their father Gilbert played the piano at the Empire in silent film days), Stan Clarke, Arthur Clarke, Leslie Noble, Roland Richards, Bill and Claude Hodges. Most were in the scout troop. For the altar servers Cyril Hircock was MC, and his assistant Bill Simms, later headmaster at the school. Other personalities were Peter Luck, Mr. Sykes, Sid Abbott, Reg Abbott and Ray Knight.

The sheer enthusiasm at St. Mary's is shown by Fred Blount's regular attendance as a young man at the 6 am service before work to act as thurifer. This continued until after his marriage to Nora Billings, a teacher at the schools. They moved to Roundhill Road, and Fred, who was building up his business as a plumber and heating engineer, was late for the service twice, so that Mr. Aveling, the verger, who was in his 80s, had to deputise for him. This troubled Fred, who felt he had to move to a nearer church, choosing St. Michael's and later SS Peter and Paul, where later in life he and Ken Bacon served for 10 years as churchwardens with Canon Pearce: "We were involved in the restoration programme whch raised many thousands of pounds, and a lot of good work was accomplished." As a practical man Fred took charge of re-leading the roof of the south aisle.

He well remembers that day he gave Fr. Rokeby two black eyes: "He arranged a match on the annual outing to Rushton, and he was very fond of an old bat with a piece knocked out of the blade. I was bowling on a bumpy pitch in the farmer's field, and the ball just seemed to run up the bat when he took a swipe at it, catching him straight between the eyes. Next morning was Sunday, and he just had to explain it when he appeared in the pulpit."

Fr. Rokeby carried on the parish for some time after Fr. Glaister's death, and often spoke of him with admiration as a saintly man and a very demanding boss, whose untimely death had been a very great loss. In his memory Fr. Rokeby provided the high altar crucifix and candlesticks. They had been made by Mr. W. F. Knight, the ecclesiastical metal expert of Wellingborough, for a cathedral in New York which found that it could not afford the import duty.

In contrast to Fr. Glaister, who spent his early years in London parishes, his successor Fr. Douglas Cooper had worked in the industrial Midlands and Potteries. As a deacon he served at St. Stephen's, Birmingham, after Durham University, then as a priest he was at St. Patrick's, Bardesley, St. Oswald's College, Ellesmere, and St. Swithin's, Worcester, holding curacies, before becoming vicar of St. Chad, Longton from 1920-1930, when he came to St. Mary's.

He maintained the pattern of worship, and at first he pursued the project of a campanile as a memorial to Fr. Glaister, but when this was ruled out by cost he suggested the beautiful chapel of Christ the King, designed by J. A. Gotch and containing many features as memorials to members of the congregation, which was added to the church instead. He was known for his long sermons, and used to say "I preach the Catholic faith as a Nonconformist."

Effie Panther wrote of him: "He was a kindly man, not exactly inspiring, and he could always fall back on the Trinity for his sermons. He was large and cumbersome, with curly locks which tended to fall over one eye, and his wife had been a dancer, so that her contribution to socials took the form of a dance. She tried to introduce a cabaret and new fangled ideas, which rather took the folk of that time by surprise. Another slight surprise rippled through the congregation when it was known that she was having another baby, when her husband seemed so old."

Though Fr. Rokeby had strong pacifist views, during the war Fr. Cooper invited him to return from Stranraer and Portpatrick, where he was priest-in-charge, to preach at a servers festival. He expressed his views, and after the service was surrounded by some hostile and vocal female critics, but a number of uniformed servicemen and women who had been in the congregation escorted him safely to his next engagement at the schools.

The war led to his marriage. Miss Elizabeth Forsyth, engaged in military censorship, was billeted on him and his housekeeper at Stranraer. They became friends, and married in 1942. Both families had been friendly with Vera Brittain. Denys's mother Lucy was 94 when she died in 1957, he died in 1969 aged 65, leaving his body to Cambridge University for research, and Elizabeth passed on in 1991 aged 87. Geoff Bellamy helped to sort out his papers, which showed that he had helped several youngsters to get to university and theological college.

His hobby from boyhood had been his collection of picture postcards. Geoff says that every spare space in his house at Barrow, Suffolk, to which he retired, contained shelves holding his albums, estimated to contain well over 100,000 cards and his own photographs.

The National Monuments Record at Swindon acquired the railway collection after his death, and the scenic subjects went to Birmingham Central Library where they are held for research and exhibitions.

Every morning at seven, before the factory hooters sounded, the Angelus bell rang from St. Mary's. It was lovingly rung by James Charles Aveling, who took over as verger in 1934 and served for 23 years until in his late 80s. He was a distinguished member of an important Fenland family, settled in Kettering in the 1920s, and in the words of Effie Panther "supervised all the happenings at St. Mary's." Congregation members were aware that they had an exceptional man in their midst, but few knew his full story.

He was born into the golden age of Fen skaters in 1869, son of a sizeable farmer at Elm, Cambridgeshire, who served as Lord

Lieutenant for that county. After schooldays at Shrewsbury he continued as a cricketer and skater, determined to excel on the ice. At the slightest frost he skated on the narrow drains to ensure the upright style that became his hallmark. In 1891 he finished 4th in the national skating championship, then beat the champion in a race at Wisbech. He won the next championship in 1892-3, as British champion took part in world championship contests, and was the foremost skater of his generation, holding many national records, some of which stood for over 50 years. His skates were made by Henie, father of Sonje the famous figure skater.

His career gradually ended, but he went on to play cricket, facing such redoubtables as Grace, Ranji, Hobbs, and other famous names on the pitch at Estover which his father provided for March CC. In one game the family doctor ran on to the pitch to call him to see a 10lb son his wife Florence had just produced, but he was needed as a bowler, and Drake-like decided to finish the game. In 1914 he was commissioned, commanded the 3rd Volunteer Battalion of the Cambridgeshire Regiment, and retired as a captain.

The between-wars agricultural depression forced him to give up farming, and he moved to Kettering, taking a greengrocery business. On country rounds by bicycle he grew to love Northamptonshire churches, and so became St. Mary's verger.

His son Bob pictures "the pleasure people found in just seeing him and Mother walking arm in arm along Stamford Road to and from church." The famous Aveling style as a skater so impressed Effie that she wrote about it: "Once when the Wicksteed Lake was frozen over I saw him with his arms folded sailing along on the ice, and I just could not understand what propelled him."

Unique among the assistant priests because of the work he did for both Canterbury and Rome at different stages in his career was the Rev. Ralph Edward Underwood, a West Haddon native who became a Durham MA and served as a curate 1914-19 at St. Mary's under Fr. Glaister. He then went to St. Margaret's, Toxteth Park, Liverpool, where he knew the Rokeby connections, and was appointed vicar of Brigstock-with-Stanion in 1928.

In 1930 he suddenly disappeared, causing something of a sensation and his whereabouts remained a mystery until news emerged that he was in Rome, had ceased to be an Anglican clergyman, and had joined the Roman Catholic Curch. After an interval he became a priest.

At that time, in the years of severe depression, Brigstock Camp was established for unemployed men from the North, who came to work in forestry and were accommodated in big army-style huts beside the Stanion road. Many of them were RCs. They created a chapel in one of the huts, asked for a priest to look after them, and Fr. Underwood was appointed, so returning to his old parish under new colours.. When Corby developed he was placed in charge of the new parish of Our Lady of Walsingham. The first church was a hut provided by Stewarts and Lloyds, from which Fr. Underwood set about building the spectacular new church and schools.

Mrs. Mary McGuinness remembers him well, describing him as a wonderful man, dedicated to his parish and a hard worker. Money to build the church came from the generosity of the new parishioners who were settling in Corby to take jobs in the steel and tube works, living in new houses that swiftly covered the rural landscape. A practical man, Fr. Underwood was friendly at all levels with Richmond Bros., the church builders, was thoroughly interested and used to climb the scaffolding to see how the job was progressing.

She adds: "He was the forefather of the whole parish. The school was built during the war because of the great need for it. Special permission was given, and reclaimed bricks had to be used. The parishioners were his family, and he had great rapport with the people during the ten years he was here. The congregations were enlarged by the presence of Italian prisoners, who were marched to Mass and had a beautiful choir. Fr. Underwood was a thoroughly nice and kind man, and we were very disappointed when he was transferred to Wellingborough."

I do not think he was able to survive his move from Corby, a parish which had been his life, for it was not long before he left the Roman Catholic Church and returned to his original fold, the Church of England. Crockford's Clerical (C of E) Directory, from which he disappeared in 1930 showed him from 1950-53 as curate at St. Paul's, Chiswick, at the same time as the Catholic Directory listed him as being on sick leave, c/o Bishop's House, Northampton.

I heard about his return to the Established Church, and his

marriage from friends at Rothwell, where before the war Mr. Burgess, a builder and an amateur astronomer, erected a full scale observatory with a revolving roof and a splendid astronomical telescope from which he allowed me to look at the moon. Revisiting Rothwell after some years I found that the observatory had gone, and inquired as to its fate. The mystery was soon solved. After his return to the Church of England Fr. Underwood had married Mrs. Burgess, his cousin, who had been left a widow, and when they moved the observatory was taken down.

From Chiswick Fr. Underwood was appointed rector of Whitstone, a parish of 360 souls six miles from the sea in west Cornwall. He held the living from 1953 until 1961, when he retired and went to live in Laura Grove, Paignton, dying there in the 1970s.

As may be expected, those who have written about St. Mary's have paid tribute to the influence for good the church and school had on them in later life. "I acquired a moral code, admittedly absorbed through fear besides desire," says David Bradshaw, who was a pupil at the school, "but I can see clearly now, half a century later, that it was here that my strength of character, my sense of decency and responsibility to others was reinforced. The experience has served me well through life, and I am a strong believer today." In an earlier generation at the school, Dorothy Woollard remembers that "religion played a large part, and we had to be able to write the creed, the ten commandments, and pieces from the catechism. We had to attend church on occasions, and were taught reading, writing, arithmetic, sewing, posture, manners and cleanliness."

Effie Panther, reflecting on St. Mary's people she knew, says "They and their families were all good people, and whether they knew it or not had an influence on the younger folk. Stability was the order of the day, and one never heard of divorce, or living together, or one's 'partner.' I am glad to have been brought up at St. Mary's."

Jack Payne, who was to see much action with the Royal Engineers, reflects "I found that the years at St. Mary's gave me comfort in the terrible years that were to follow, and through it all I never doubted that there is a God, and that he was with me at all times."

When St. Mary's church building reached its centenary on 9 February 1995, parishioners who wished to visit Sulby to renew thanks in spirit to Lady Elizabeth could not do so. The Hall, built in 1795 to the design of Sir John Soane, had long gone, demolished in 1948.

THE SUNDAY PROMENADE

In a vivid survey of the Free Churches when he was young, David Bradshaw provides a welcome companion chapter to the one on St. Mary's. The churches and church life in general contributed much to the vitality of Kettering, he says. Their influence pervaded professions and pastimes, and there was ample rivalry between the denominations.

There were geographical areas of influence. For example, the top of Gold Street, in those days the centre of business and commercial life, was dominated by the grey bulk of Fuller Church with its steep steps and wrought iron railings. At the other end of the street was the turbulent territory of Toller Church, led at one time by the Rev. Keith Doman, a go-getting young preacher whose youthful flock could be seen every Sunday evening in groups around Bakehouse Hill. They had hymn books clamped beneath their arms, but the obvious principal purpose of their endeavour was to pursue the mating game:

"I hasten to add that the term had a very different connotation from that of today. When the talkative twosomes had sorted themselves out they would parade to the other end of Gold Street, force a passage through the much larger crowd of Fuller Baptists of whom many were engaged in exactly the same exercise, turn right through Dalkeith Place, and if it was a fine summer evening they might even reach Wicksteed Park before they so much as held hands. On reflection, a better description would be the meeting game."

Halfway through this Sunday evening circuit the promenaders would encounter two more groups, first those coming out of London Road Congregational Church, and then past Speight's Corner the Catholics leaving their newly-built and impressive St. Edward's.

David reflects: "A major pleasure in going to chapel, church or citadel in those days was enjoyed afterwards. The end of a summer evening service was the signal for a social extension which began with handshakes for the departing flock, continued with gossiping clusters in front of the building, and ended with a walk, making appointments, and promising to meet again the next Sunday. The power of faith in the 1930s and 1940s was evidenced by vast numbers of followers, united in their belief in God though divided by their ways of worship.''

David walks back to take a special look at the Methodists in School Lane, where stood the Tordoff Sunday School, a rambling building used during the week for union branch meetings, collecting dues for sick and coal clubs, parties and wedding receptions: ''But on Sundays the Tordoff was for worship only. There was an infants school and a junior school staffed by devout young men and women who shepherded their innocent flocks for an hour or two in the afternoon.

''Classes were quite simple. After a hymn or two and a prayer beneath the protective gaze of St. Francis surrounded by birds and animals, the class would read a passage from the Bible and be told a story to explain its import, always with the aim of instilling a moral. It was a general introduction to Christianity, a moral code for life, and a study of the Bible. Bible classes were immensely popular for teenagers and those in their early twenties. Two names which come to mind are Mrs. Morris and Miss Butcher whose Bible classes both fielded football teams.''

Also on Sunday afternoons across the road in the Methodist Church, David recalls, was a unique institution which attracted believers from all denominations and agnostics as well: ''This was the Men's and Women's Own, always an uplifting occasion. It was more a concert than a service. The building resembled a theatre more than a church, with gleaming rows of seats, cream walls and clear glass windows allowing the sunlight to flood in.

''The presiding master of ceremonies was Mr. Charles Saunders, a layman. He was old – I believe he carried out these duties until well into his eighties – and he sat on a wooden chair, facing and beaming at his happy congregation, whom he often moved to laughter and applause – both unheard of in churches then. As I remember it, the jovial and extremely lovable Mr. Saunders took one of the ladies of his audience, also in her eighties, as his bride towards the end of his life. My grandmother,

Mary Elizabeth Bradshaw, was a regular supporter, and when telling her of his marriage intentions he added 'Of course, it is purely for companionship.' ''

Best of all, David continues, the Men's and Women's Own had a splendid orchestra led by violinist Mr. Inns. It accompanied hymns and played overtures, marches and descriptive works, with the most popular ones ''In a Monastery Garden'' and ''Bells Across the Meadows'' which gave percussionist Vince Garlick every opportunity to introduce bird calls and animal noises. Mr. Saunders, head swaying to the music, would conduct with a commanding index finger:

''This was religion with a spring in its step. All the musicians were familiar and popular figures, some solo performers, others members of dance bands or brass bands, or stars at club concerts or receptions, for which they were paid. But at the Men's and Women's Own their services were free.''

Charles Saunders was a glutton for good work. He was also president of the Victoria Hall Mission, a similar gathering which after the old 'Vic' theatre became a cinema moved to Tordoff School and met on Sunday evenings.

Another outstanding personality was the Rev. Leonard Wide, whom David describes as a flamboyant Maurice Chevalier lookalike. Arriving in the 1930s, he was portly, good-looking and dapper, and often preferred a speckled bow tie to a dog collar. He was an erudite and accomplished speaker, a splendid raconteur, and when the time came to preach he would on occasions leave the pulpit, descend majestically to the front of the church and stand defiantly as if daring anyone to fail to give their full attention:

Charles Saunders was the presiding genius of the Men's and Women's Own, an unofficial church which filled the Central Methodist building on Sunday afternoons. Charles attracted a volunteer orchestra which led the best known hymns and concert singers gave their services. As one of his congregation said: "this was Christianity with a spring in its step."
(Kettering Council).

"For twenty or thirty minutes he would analyse and explain a particular topic without notes, and his stories were renowned. He delighted in recounting his conversation with Gandhi on a train in India, and trains had a hand in his marriage. He was in a London-bound express when another roared by, going in the opposite direction. Suddenly amid the blur of passing windows he caught a glimpse of the most beautiful eyes he vowed he had ever seen. On arrival in London the bemused young man had no alternative but to take the next train back in pursuit of the bewitching eyes. He found them, and married their owner within a few short weeks."

Eventually Leonard Wide and London Road Church followed different paths. After a time as volunteer welfare officer for clothing manufacturers Wallis and Linnell he "left the church altogether and became the full-time personnel officer for the firm. I believe he was past ninety when he was called to meet the Master he had sought to serve in such unorthodox ways."

Casting his mind back to the 'thirties, 'forties and 'fifties, David maintains that for many people their church was not just a Sunday affair. Far from it. For many it was a daily preoccupation. Churches had halls attached, used every evening of the week for badminton, folk dancing, choir practice, amateur dramatics, table tennis, Scouts, Cubs, Guides, St. John Ambulance, and other guests:

"I loved all the weekly activities of my church and so did all my friends, many of whom were my companions by day at Kettering Grammar School. Of course there was another interest, because although the Grammar School and girls' High school shared the Bowling Green Road building lessons were so cunningly arranged that boys and girls never met. But at London Road Church Institute we could fraternise as much as we wished, although always well chaperoned.

"I enjoyed immensely the summer walks we sometimes organised on Sunday evenings to visit village nonconformist churches at Geddington and Broughton and lend our support to their congregations. Best of all I loved summer strolls after Sunday evening services to Rockingham Road Park. There we would meet our friends from the Rockingham Road churches, Fuller, Toller, and Bath Road Primitive Methodists, gather round the beautiful bandstand and listen to some eminent brass band – our favourites

Munn and Felton's or Rushden Temperance.

"Whenever in nostalgic mood I find myself sitting in my garden watching the sunset across my beautiful Lincolnshire landscape, my mind inevitably turns to one particular evening when, as I approached the Park I heard the strains of the Destiny Waltz on the summer air, and I knew I was in love – with a girl, with life, and with God."

THE 'BLAZING CAR MURDER'

The 'Blazing Car Murder' occurred on the night of 5-6 November, 1930. A car was found on fire near Hardingstone with a body inside it. The owner, who had fled the scene, was Alfred Arthur Rouse, who was charged with murder, found guilty and hanged. The prosecution's case was that Rouse, who wanted to disappear, selected a man without relatives or friends, killed him and incinerated his body in the car in the hope that it would be mistaken for his own, which would enable him to vanish and start a new life.

The motive, it was suggested, was Rouse's expensive involvement with women. Evidence for this was produced at the police court preliminary hearing, but was not pursued at Northamptonshire Assizes as it was considered inadmissible. Rouse's defence was that he had picked up a hitch hiker whom he did not know, and that the fatal fire was an accident.

The case was for many months a national sensation with local connections, doubt being thrown on the fairness of the legal procedure and on the genuineness of condemned cell "confessions." Eventually the case was discussed in the Commons and the Lords because of its highly unusual features.

It has many times been written about, but it was not a simple open-and-shut case, as is shown here with information from cuttings, notes and memories. The account typifies the murder cases that were such a dramatic and macabre feature of life before the death penalty for murder was abolished in 1965.

I well remember the impact of the Rouse case on the *Evening Telegraph*, where I had just finished my first year. The district had been mercifully free from murders, and at first the discovery of a body in a blazing car at Hardingstone seemed to be an accident, but within hours the event changed character and became one of the classic murder cases. I still recall the note of surprise in freelance Jim Purvis's voice when he rang us with the news "Rouse has been charged with murder."

At intervals the story filled many columns of the then broadsheet paper, and though the proceedings were at Northampton, three of the police officers closely concerned, Superintendents Tebbey and Brumby and PC (later Superintendent) Copping were all well known in Kettering, serving here at various times. I was one of a relay of people taking down from our candlestick-type telephone full accounts of the proceedings at Northampton police court and Assizes from Jim who at intervals came puffing across the Square from the court to his office in the Arcade buildings.

The story began at 11.15 that Bonfire Night. A policeman in Markyate noticed a Morris Minor, MU 1468, standing on the road with its lights out. This was an offence then, so PC David Lilley shone his torch on the occupants, two men. The passenger explained that he had switched the lights off accidentally, they were switched on again and the officer dismissed the matter with a word of caution, also noting it. To understand what follows, one must recall the design of the 1930 Morris Minor. It was a two-door fabric saloon, with the front seats tipping forward to let passengers into the back. The petrol tank was positioned under the scuttle and above the passenger's lap, the petrol pipe passed through the space above his feet on its way to the carburettor, and was fixed at each end by screw union brass nuts – in the case of MU 1468 nuts destined before many weeks had passed to be exhaustively discussed by some of the most distinguished legal brains in the country.

After PC Lilley's investigation the Morris went on its way towards Leicester. The driver was Rouse who lived in Finchley, worked as a traveller at £4 a week plus expenses for a Leicester braces and suspenders firm, used the car for his business, was buying it on the never-never, and was on his way to the firm's office to draw cash due to him.

Rouse was later described as living a Jekyll and Hyde existence at his suburban home. Regarded by neighbours as a conventional business man, he was really living several secret lives elsewhere with one bogusly-wed wife and other women who had borne him children. His legal wife was aware of his entanglements, but had stopped asking questions. He had started work as an office boy in a warehouse, joined the Army four days after the outbreak of war in 1914, and was discharged in 1916 with a pension after being severely wounded in the head. The injury was said to have altered his character as regards women. When travelling he became a dashing debonair lover, representing himself as single and leaving a trail of young women duped into regarding him as fiance or husband. He told police "At times I have difficulty in holding myself down."

Rouse's passenger in the Morris, destined to die a most unpleasant death that night, was never identified. Rouse himself had but four months to live before he would fall to his death in the hangman's noose at Bedford gaol.

The ill-starred pair carried on driving north, and after passing through Hardingstone, off the direct route, Rouse pulled up at the side of the road. It was after two in the morning. What happened next only the two men would ever know. Rouse's story was that he left the car to relieve himself and asked the passenger to fill up the petrol tank from a two-gallon can while he had gone. To make this easier he lifted the bonnet over the tank filler cap, and left the full petrol can on the driver's seat after loosening its screw cap with a mallet. The man had asked for and been given cigarettes, matches and a cigar, and had drunk from a bottle of whisky.

While relieving himself some distance away, Rouse thought he heard the car self-starter, and then saw an appalling glare. The Morris was a mass of flames. First, he said, he went to open the car door, but could not approach it because of the heat. He ran towards the village shouting, then simply wanted to get away from the scene of horror. He picked up his attache case and made for the main road.

It was then that he encountered the Hardingstone men, Bill Bailey and Alf Brown coming home from a dance, but instead of running to them and asking their help he casually shouted "It looks as if somebody has got a bonfire up there," and went on his way. At the main road he got a lift in a lorry and disappeared.

The two men went to the blazing car, then knocked up PC Copping and parish constable Hedley Bailey. They organised buckets to put out the fire, PC Copping summoned help from Northampton, and the police lifted the remains of the passenger from his funeral pyre and took them to an empty garage at the Crown Inn, Hardingstone. Sir Bernard Spilsbury the Home Office pathologist was called in to conduct a post-mortem, and removed specimens for analysis.

Meanwhile the police had set up a hue and cry for Rouse, identified from his car number plate which had survived, and whose behaviour after the tragedy did not help him at his trial. The lorry driver took him to London, where he first visited his wife, then bought a new Stetson to replace the hat he had left in the car, and hung about on the Embankment looking for a coach to Cardiff. A porter working for one of the transport firms thought he looked dazed, befriended him, and saw him on to a coach. Rouse travelled to a South Wales village where he was friendly with a family whose daughter, pregnant by him, was known as Mrs. Rouse. He had been in the habit of staying there from Thursday to Monday each week.

He told the family that his car had been stolen but next day things took a sinister turn when national newspapers arrived carrying pictures of the burnt-out Morris and stating that the police had identified Rouse as the owner and were seeking him. At first Rouse denied that the car was his, then decided to make a rapid exit, getting a lift into Cardiff and taking a coach back to London.

The lift was given him by a man whose suspicions were aroused, and who informed the police of his movements. As a result he was met off the coach at Hammersmith and taken to the police station, where he was questioned by four police officers who included Superintendent Brumby and Inspector Lawrence of the Northamptonshire police. The interview, during the night, went on for four hours. Rouse, who had said when leaving the coach "I am responsible. I am glad it is all over", seemed eager to tell his story, and maintained that he had been on his way to Scotland Yard to provide details about the car blaze. The officers said he was treated with every courtesy, but they were not convinced he was telling the truth, mainly because he made so many minor corrections to his statement.

Rouse was detained, charged by Superintendent Brumby with the murder of an unknown man, and on 10 November appeared at the police court before Northampton magistrates, pleading not guilty. Aged 36, handsome and even striking in appearance, he was well built, of medium height, and throughout the proceedings faced the magistrates with his dark hair brushed back, his small moustache neatly trimmed, and his hands manicured. He wore a smart brown suit, and carried a double-breasted raincoat and leather gauntlets. His undoubted sex appeal was reflected in newspaper pictures, and there were amazing scenes outside the court, crowds of women and girls blocking the road as they tried to get into the building or at least catch a glimpse of him.

When he first appeared he complained that the police seemed to want him to look as disreputable as possible, lending him a suit with sleeves much too short, and he needed a change of clothing. Superintendent Tebbey said his clothes were under examination, but there was no objection to his having others from home, which were brought.

It was claimed that at the outset severe damage was done to Rouse's defence by the procedure then followed, which in recent years has been altered by reporting restrictions. In those days it was permissible for the prosecution's case to be fully reported at the magistrates court, while the accused merely pleaded not guilty and reserved his defence for the Assizes. So it was that Rouse's extra-marital adventures were revealed in newspapers all over the country, with sensational headlines and news placards, but this evidence was omitted from the Crown case at the Assizes, the Crown deciding in the interval that it was inadmissible. Guidance on this aspect of law was given many years earlier by Lord Herschel to the effect that it was not competent for the prosecution to show that the accused had been guilty of acts other than those covered in the indictment.

It was claimed that the case received so much publicity that the Assizes jury could not have been unaware of allegations made before the magistrates imputing a motive for murder, though not put before them during the trial. The magistrates court evidence in question came from three women witnesses. A probationer nurse said she had given birth to a child fathered by Rouse and was receiving money from him for an earlier child. A father from Wales gave evidence of Rouse's relationship with his daughter whom he had ''married'' in a bogus ceremony. A Kent waitress said she had borne two children by Rouse.

Police evidence was that Rouse had said ''My harem takes me

to several places – it is an expensive game", and from these facts it was suggested that it would have been no great inconvenience to Rouse if the body in the car had been mistaken for him, so that he could have disappeared.

Mr. D. L. Finnemore, defending, complained that the women's evidence brought to the case an enormous amount of prejudice: "Does it prove, or help anybody to prove, that he committed a murder? There is no evidence that he ever made a single preparation for such an act. He does not attempt to disappear, vanish or hide himself."

At the Assizes a feature of the trial was the clash between Rouse's evidence that the fire was accidental, and the prosecution's allegation that Rouse rendered his victim unconscious and then soaked him in petrol and started the fire. A vital piece of evidence was the position of the body in the burnt out car, but without photographs or drawings this depended on the memories of witnesses. Inspector Lawrence said that the body was lying across the front seats, the head on the driver's seat face down, the trunk on the passenger's seat. The right leg extended to just outside the car, the right foot was burnt off, the left leg was doubled up under the body, the right arm extended to the height of the passenger's seat, and the left leg was not visible.

Sir Bernard Spilsbury considered that the body would have been stiffened by the fire and its position was consistent with being thrown face downward on the seats from the nearside door. The man had breathed for about half a minute before death from shock due to burns. The clothing was soaked in petrol. He did not agree that the man had been trying to get out of the driver's door, and considered that the passenger's door was open during the fire so that the right leg could extend beyond where the door was. Called by the defence, Dr. R. B. Wyatt, pathologist at Bedford Hospital thought a possibility was that the man was trying to get out and stretched out his right arm to open the driver's door. He would do this if the fire was by the passenger's door.

On Sir Bernard's evidence, Norman Birkett for the Crown suggested that Rouse had rendered the man unconscious, threw him into the car in the position in which he was found, and lit the petrol. Rouse denied this, saying that he had no idea how to knock a man out. It was agreed that no improper use had been made of a mallet found at the scene.

A great deal of play was made by both sides about the car's petrol union nuts being found loose after the fire. The prosecution alleged that Rouse had loosened one or both to provide petrol to feed the fire. It must have come as a suprise to Norman Birkett when two people experienced in car fires came voluntarily to give evidence that they had found the nuts loose after fires. This prompted the famous Birkett question "What is the coefficient of expansion of brass?" The first witness was taken aback and could not answer, which made it appear to the jury that he was not the expert he claimed to be, but the second was unperturbed saying that he did not need to know the figure, and he could easily look it up.

Mr. Justice Talbot summed up without indicating where he thought the stronger argument lay. There was no plausible theory as to any motive for murder, he said. If the jury were satisfied that a murder was committed, it was not their business to inquire why. After a 13 minute retirement the jury returned a unanimous verdict of guilty. Rouse said "I am not guilty, sir," before the judge donned the black cap and pronounced sentence of death, but the drama was far from over. Rouse appealed, and leading for the defence before the Lord Chief Justice (Lord Hewart), Mr. Justice Avory and Mr. Justice Humphreys was Sir Patrick Hastings, a former Attorney General whose wide experience outside the law may have given him sympathy with Rouse, as they were both old soldiers. He said that a friend paid his fee, but he may well have done the work for nothing, as he did in another famous case.

Sir Patrick was on his feet for two and a half hours pleading for Rouse's life. Rouse had been convicted on prejudice and suspicion, he said. No motive was established, and Rouse's character had been blazoned abroad in such a way as to arouse horror. Dreadful results came from unwarrantable evidence at the police court, so that he stood his trial in an atmosphere of unreasonable and unreasoning prejudice. Sir Patrick wanted to call fresh evidence about the loose petrol union nuts, as he could now prove that they were inevitably found loose after fires, but the judges refused the request. He submitted that conviction for murder must rest not on suspicion but proof, and he thought the trial judge ought to have withdrawn the case from the jury.

For the Crown, Norman Birkett said that the facts proved to

the jury were the occasion of Rouse's journey, the time and place of the fire, the burning beyond recognition of an unknown man, and the fact that Rouse rendered no assistance and instead of staying and reporting went away and made excuses for two days.

Lord Hewart, dismissing the appeal, said the only ground for it would have been that there was no case to go to the jury, and the judges considered this an impossible contention.

Rouse, with his three warders about him, stumbled blindly out of sight before many people in court realised that he had gone. Half an hour later, an incongruous dark-suited figure wearing bowler hat and spats, he was hurried out to a prison van on his way back to the condemned cell at Bedford gaol. Observers at the Law Courts declared that scenes witnessed during the hearing had been without precedent. Fashionably-dressed women, barristers and others took part in struggles at the two entrances to the court, literally fighting for admission. There were tears in Rouse's eyes as he took his last look at the London scene. Permission to appeal to the House of Lords was refused, as no point of law of exceptional public importance was involved.

Interest in the case continued unabated in the newspapers. Next day the *Daily Herald* published a statement from Major General Sir Wyndham Childs who from 1921-28 had served as Assistant Commissioner Metropolitan Police and head of the CID. Under the heading ROUSE SHOULD NOT HANG he wrote: "No matter how fair the trial and how convincing the evidence, the fact remains that through the lamentable indiscretion of the Crown in tendering evidence before the magistrates that was not brought at the Assizes the jury must have been prejudiced – as every citizen must be prejudiced today against this man.

"The Law has been incapable of righting a wrong which the Law produced. Such being the case, let the Crown intervene where the officers of the Crown erred. In other words, let the Home Secretary invoke the Royal Prerogative and spare the life of Rouse in order that justice may be done." Sir Wyndham's view was supported by the paper's leading article, which maintained that there was a clear case for not hanging Rouse.

Interviewed in the same issue, Mrs. Rouse said "Whatever happens now, I shall still believe in Arthur." One of the women friends who gave evidence said "He was too gentle and kind to have committed such a terrible crime," and the other commented

"I still believe that Arthur is innocent of murder. I loved him as a wife for ten years, and I love him still." It was revealed that one of the women had been to the Home Office with additional information about the burned-out car. The near side door handle and fittings were found inside the wreck, indicating that the passenger door had been closed as Dr. Wyatt thought.

Mrs. Rouse made a direct appeal to Mrs. Clynes, wife of the Home Secretary, who told the Press "I was sitting quietly at home when my telephone rang. It was Mrs. Rouse, the poor soul, asking for me. I went straight to the phone and talked to her and tried to comfort her, for she was so terribly distressed. It was really pitiful. I was frightfully sorry for her, but explained as gently as I could that I was powerless to do anything for her. I can do nothing in a case like this. Mrs. Rouse was so upset that she could hardly speak. She thanked me very much in a broken voice for answering her call and said that she wanted to appeal to me as one woman to another to do whatever I could. 'Please help my husband,' she said, 'I know he is innocent.' I advised her to appeal direct to the Home Office and I know my husband received a pathetic appeal from her in a telegram. It is all so sad for her. Everyone must be very sorry."

The *News Chronicle* explained WHY ROUSE WAS NOT REPRIEVED in a news item stating that the Home Secretary was greatly impressed at the public feeling aroused and spent two whole days examining the evidence, documents, and other matters to do with the case, besides consulting Mr. Justice Talbot and the Lord Chief Justice: "The complete absence of comment by Mr. Justice Talbot when he passed sentence, and the idea that his summing-up appeared to favour the accused has led to the belief that he did not agree with the verdict. The fact that Mr. Clynes was in full possession of the judges' views before he refused the reprieve would appear to dispose of doubt on this point."

The *Evening Telegraph* reported events on the eve and day of the execution, 10 March. "Rouse bade farewell to his wife with the words 'Goodbye, dear. You are the best woman I have ever known. I hope the future will hold greater happiness for you.' Mrs. Rouse asked that the interview should be interrupted so that her husband could see one of his women friends. After they had said farewell Mrs. Rouse returned, as it was her husband's wish that she should be the last to see him.

"She concealed her grief until out of sight of her husband. Then she collapsed and was carried to a car. During the last hours she was with friends, and remained in seclusion during the time of the execution. She spent today quietly, and after another week or two will leave for an unknown destination, there to begin life afresh, probably under another name."

The paper reported on events that morning outside Bedford Gaol: "From chimneys behind the high walls the smoke of early-morning fires rose straight into the clear sky. The street on which the massive prison gates open was deserted until half past seven, when it began to fill with people. The governor left his house and entered the gates, to be followed by the doctor and the chaplain. Slowly the hands of the clock on Trinity Church moved round. With ten minutes to wait the crowd increased rapidly to several hundred, marshalled by police into ranks. Women and young girls formed the majority. Inside, the little procession from the condemned cell to the scaffold would be forming.

"The winter sun had risen. Overhead wheeled a flock of pigeons. There remained only a few seconds. The crowd stirred uneasily, eyes on the clock. The first stroke of eight boomed out, and moved by a sudden impulse of pity the crowd fell quiet. Women bowed their heads and every man removed his hat. The clock was still striking as from somewhere in the crowd a woman began sobbing. Alfred Arthur Rouse had paid for his crime.

"Then there was a rasping of bolts, a wicket door opened, and two warders came out, quickly attaching two black notice boards to the door. One, signed by the under-sheriff for Northamptonshire, the governor and the chaplain declared that judgement of death had been executed. The other from the prison surgeon certified death. A little later a third notice signed by the coroner and jurors stated that an inquest was held, death was instantaneous, the drop was 5ft 4in, and the executioner and deputy were Pierrepoint and Philips."

That might have been the end of the story, but the day after the execution the *Daily Sketch* carried this surprising case a stage further by publishing what it claimed to be ROUSE'S FULL MURDER CONFESSION. The article, written in the first person prompted the question as to how more than 1,000 words could have been written or dictated by Rouse, who was always closely watched by warders. Nothing was offered in support, such as a few lines of Rouse's writing with his signature, and the confession was challenged later. It was of no value, as apart from the question of its genuineness it repeated the evidence given in court and gave no description of any convincing plan by Rouse as to how he meant to vanish.

Describing the murder it stated "I gripped him by the throat with my right hand. People have always said that I have a terrific grip. He did not resist. After making a peculiar noise the man was silent and I thought he was dead or unconscious."

He then poured petrol over the man according to the statement, loosened the union joint, laid a trail of petrol to the car, put the can in the back of the car, and struck a match. The whole

Controversial articles about the Rouse case were still occupying public attention long after his execution for the 'blazing car murder.' John Bull was concerned about the genuineness of 'confessions.' Rouse is shown here with his wife and one of his women friends.

thing was a mass of flames in seconds. He intended to walk through Northampton and get a train to Scotland, but changed his plans after meeting the two Hardingstone men. He went to Wales because he had to go somewhere, and then back to London because of its size. He never asked the name of the man burned in the car.

It was an even greater sensation when on Sunday 15 March the *News of the World* devoted its front page to a statement from Mrs. Rouse, in the form of a facsimile of her handwriting signed by her:

THE PROOF OF ROUSE'S GUILT

I have fought to the last ditch to save my husband's life. But alas I have failed and the law will take its course.

Those who knew Arthur will know the good that was in him. I did, and so do others.

But I knew I was fighting a lost cause, for before he went to the Court of Criminal Appeal he had told me that the jury's verdict was the correct one, and he was guilty.

My own opinion is that he was not in his right mind on November 5th.

Lily May Rouse

March 7, 1931

This amazing turn about by Mrs. Rouse, whose sincerity had never seemed in question as she struggled tenaciously to save her husband, caused such a ferment that within a few days the controversy reached Parliament. In the Commons on 16 March the Home Secretary was asked if he would inquire how Rouse's purported confession reached the Press. Mr. Clynes replied that he had made searching inquiries and was satisfied that no confession was passed out by any official, and he thought it very unlikely that one was sent out in any other way. He could not answer for the resources or inventiveness of the Press. Statements purporting to describe the last hours of Rouse, where they did not relate to matters of ordinary routine were sheer fabrication.

A feeling of outrage at some of the newspaper articles was voiced in the Lords on 29 April when Lord Darling called attention to newspaper comments while the Rouse appeal was pending, to alleged confessions, and to the publication of evidence before the justices which should have been restricted. Certainly some newspapers committed contempt of court, a most grave offence. They forgot the duty of restraint, and published a great deal that was inexpedient.

The newspapers also published their views of what should be considered by the judges as to allowing or dismissing the appeal, said Lord Darling. It might be said that the judges could not be influenced as they proceeded on different principles and lived on a different level. He had been a judge, but never thought himself so raised above all human weakness, and did not think his fellow judges were either. Some of these statements were contempt of court of the most dangerous character.

There was already a remedy – the exclusion of public and Press from preliminary investigations in sensational crimes, which he believed to be good law. After the newspaper licence and misplaced liberty in this case it might be that the defendant would apply for the next one to be heard in camera. Some newspapers published what purported to be confessions. One of the worst examples was what purported to be a facsimile, exclusive to the *News of the World*, of the "he told me he was guilty" letter written by Mrs. Rouse, also referring to her husband's mental state, which Lord Darling read out with the comment "that was never laid before the jury." The House cheered when he said "Everyone must come to the conclusion that such things were done for money."

The Lord Chancellor said Lord Darling had drawn attention to a growing evil. After Rouse's conviction the *Daily Express* proclaimed that the verdict was undoubtedly right, and professed to give facts they thought had not been presented to the public because of legal difficulties. The *Daily Worker* protested that a man was being sent to the gallows on extremely flimsy circumstantial evidence, that nothing had been proved, and that without the brilliance of the prosecuting counsel the whole case would have fallen to pieces. Both articles were regrettable and unfortunate. With comments by other papers they were considered, but in view of the decision of the High Court in another case it was thought unlikely that they would be held as contempt of court.

It had been the rule of the Home Office for many years not to publish confessions, or that a confession had been made except in some exceptional cases, and in the Rouse case the Home Secretary had stated explicitly that no confession was passed out by an official.

The Lord Chancellor added that he felt that the marketing of sensational stories in connection with current criminal cases was a great evil. It was not in the interests of justice or of public morality that the sordid details of a criminal career should be spread abroad to be read by young and old alike. He appealed to editors and proprietors, and asked them whether it was desirable to discontinue publication of such articles.

The drama flickered up again on 8 May, when the magazine *John Bull*, self-styled righter of wrongs, announced that it had sent additional information to the Home Secetary, and asked that Mr. Clynes should make a further statement about Rouse's alleged confession. Three warders, it stated, were present at all interviews between Rouse and his visitors in the condemned cell. A glass partition separated him and his visitors, a warder stood on each side of him within inches, and another stood close behind the visitor's chair: "The listening warders say he never confessed, his legal advisers say so too, and so does the Home Secretary."

The magazine asked what was the explanation that Mrs. Rouse finally changed her whole story and agreed that her husband was guilty. When, where and how did he say this to her? During their last interview he told his wife "I am not guilty" and next day she was still denying that he had made any confession.

John Bull concluded: "We hope the facts we have placed before the Home Secretary will prevent any further traffic in stories about men under the shadow of the scaffold who have no means of defending themselves."

Looking back to 1930, I remember that among my section of the population Rouse was regarded as guilty even before his Assizes trial and nobody thought of speaking a word in his defence. Today we live in more humane and understanding times. With hindsight one can see that here was a man who had volunteered for the Colours within days of the 1914 war breaking out, saw service at the front and was so severely wounded that his mind was affected. Yet nothing seems to have been argued about that in his defence. As regards the blazing car death, evidence was stated in court to have been purely circumstantial, and the devotion of both Mrs. Rouse and his principal woman friend hardly suggests that he was a brute. There was no description of any plan he had to vanish after the car fire, and he did not attempt to do so. Above all, with so much advance publicity from the police court, were the Assize jury swayed by what they had read? Since then, cases have collapsed for just this reason. By present day standards Rouse was certainly not treated fairly. The question remains, was he a murderer? The jury, who saw him in court for days on end, decided that he was.

Re-reading the whole tragic story, it is evident that the noose was placed round Rouse's neck by Sir Bernard Spilsbury. When he was at the height of his fame as the leading 'detective-pathologist' his evidence was invariably accepted by juries, as the Dictionary of National Biography records, and his reconstruction of the fatal scene at Hardingstone carried the day. Seeking a parallel, I can only say that Sir Bernard dominated the real world of detection as Sherlock Holmes stands unchallenged as the great detective of fiction.

Points that might have shaken him did not emerge at the trial, such as the car door handle and fittings said to be found inside the wreck, which could have supported Dr. Wyatt's view. The loose petrol unions it seems could have been due to the heat of the fire expanding the nuts first, so that they were loosened on their seatings, and further loosened by the escaping petrol vapour. Perhaps one day someone will review the events of that night in the light of modern knowledge.

To a layman Sir Bernard's life seems overcharged with horror and drama. He conducted over 25,000 post mortem examinations and his reputation was founded on a phenomenal memory and prodigious attention to detail. He died by his own hand at 70 in 1947.

If further comment is necessary, it is provided by the Brighton trunk murders a few years later. At the trial of Tony Mancini following the discovery of women's bodies in trunks at left luggage deposits it was pointed out that there had been a lot of pre-trial publicity, as in the Rouse case. But this time Norman Birkett was defending. No doubt remembering the Rouse case he pleaded that the jury could not bring open minds to bear because of what they might have read, and Mancini walked free.

In a *Tablet* review of Lord Devlin's 1997 autobiography, Terence Morris, Emeritus Professor of Criminology and Criminal Justice at London University, says there are glimpses of some of the great figures of Devlin's time "and of others who are remembered for different reasons to this day; Mr. Justice Avory who, noticing the absence of a defendant who had been taken ill in prison, asked if they had no stretchers, and Lord Hewart, generally regarded as having no competition for the title of the worst Lord Chief Justice since the seventeenth century."

Three judges heard Rouse's appeal. Lord Hewart presided, and Mr. Justice Avory was one of the other two.

THE SOCCER SCENE

In writing about Kettering Town – the good old Poppies as most of us call them – I have an admission to make. In the 1930s I never once saw a Saturday match on the Rockingham Road ground. Before you cry "Shame", there was a good reason. Every Saturday afternoon I was deskbound, toiling to help bring out the *Football Telegraph (Pink 'Un* to its readers).

I sat with a phone glued to my ear, taking down match reports from all over the place, some phoned in by journalists, others by part-timers ranging from auctioneers to zoologists, all motivated by a love of football and a desire to get their team into print.

To co-ordinate this torrent of telephoning they all came through on booked fixed-time calls (there's a bit of GPO history for you), rushing from the game to the nearest phone box and shouting their report and score, all breathless and sweaty and usually agitated because the ref's re-start whistle was sounding in the background. From the printers' kingdom next door to me came the noise of Linotype machines (What are they, Grandad?) at full stretch, setting the type for that wonderful Saturday evening paper, so much part of Kettering's sporting history.

Well, that's my excuse for the fact that most of this chapter has been provided by good friends who did see the matches, and who have rallied round with memories. It is not an attempt at history – more a lucky dip of bits and pieces about the Poppies, which you will doubtless supplement for Book 6, if I live that long.

Anyway, to cut the cackle and get on with the 'osses, Kettering's almost boundless enthusiasm for football was evident every Saturday afternoon in the 1920s and 1930s. Philip Hague lived in Kingsley Avenue and on his way down Rockingham Road encountered the fans making for the football ground. He draws a lively picture: "Because of the crowds either going to the

Poppies' games or returning to the town, it was hardly possible for anyone bound in the opposite direction to walk along Rockingham Road just before the kick-off or after the final whistle without being swept up a side street. Sometimes there would be 4,000 spectators, nearly all arriving on foot, and the ground was so packed that bolder spirits used to climb up and sit along the corrugated iron roof of the Athletic Club.''

At different times, as permitted by their finances, Kettering played in the Southern League, the East Midland League which they won in 1926, or the Birmingham League, and were members of the Northamptonshire FA. At the same time as the Town game attracted spectators by the thousand, lower-level amateur teams all over the district were staging their own matches, cheered on by supporters. It was a gigantic soccer free-for-all, under the control of the efficiently-run Kettering and District Amateur League which had been born of a general enthusiasm for football in the early 1920s.

At that time many scratch teams were fielded by streets, villages, factories, churches and athletic groups, playing friendly games with one another. They had no facilities apart from open fields, and piled coats served as goalposts and pitch markers.

One Sunday morning Claude Patrick, Harry Adams, George Cragg the *Evening Telegraph* photographer and a few more friends were having a pint and a chat when someone produced the bright idea of organising all these amateur teams into a league.

Ted Grove says: ''Within a year the suggestion reached fruition, and the Kettering and District Junior Football League started, backed by influential businessmen and sportsmen, with George Cragg as secretary and treasurer. It was most successful, and in 1929 developed into the Amateur League which ran until 1978. During the 1930s it had three divisions.''

Dennis Wildman remembers some good sides in the Amateur League in the 1930s, among them the Junior Imps, Kettering East End, Miss Butcher's Bible Class, Fuller Institute, Freeman Hardy and Willis, and Frank Wright's. Individuals raised sides to play for charity, Fred Deeley's XI for example challenging the redoubtable LMS Railway FC, and an all-Collins team aged 14 to 50 challenged any same-name eleven. They found another all-Collins team to play. Even the unemployed ran two teams on the Northampton Road ''Rec.''

The Gasworks had a ground with the Slade brook providing water for cleaning-up after a game, and the Imps (young Conservative members of the Junior Imperial League) were based along Weekley Road opposite Grange Farm. Miss Butcher's BC always drew plenty of supporters to their pitch off Windmill Avenue behind London Road brickyard quarry, and other teams played on Wicksteed Park or the agricultural showground off Pytchley Road, now built over.

East End, says Dennis, was from its formation successful in winning many honours and grooming players for more senior teams. Notable was Maurice Dunkley, prevented by the war from becoming a name in football, and others who made their mark were Bill ("Tubby") Tite and Tommy ("Bungy") Smith, one of the best wing halves Kettering ever had. Dennis pays tribute to those tireless workers the club secretaries, backbone of local teams: "It usually fell to the home team secretary to define the playing area – no small job unaided. He would cycle to Lewis's timber shed in Hallwood Road, collect a sack of sawdust, then go to the ground and use the sawdust to mark out the pitch."

Many of the Kettering Town stars shine brightly in memory, led by left back Eddie Hapgood, acquired in the late 'twenties by Arsenal. "This was a great opportunity," says Ted Grove. "He served them very well through the 1930s until the war, when he was called into the RAF and became sports officer controlling the RAF's requirements, eventually moving up to take charge of the whole of BAOR's sporting facilities."

Ted had close contact with Kettering Town, as his father George was secretary when the club was in the Southern League, taking on teams from London and the Home Counties. The Poppies usually gave a good account of themselves, though on the business side financial peaks and troughs alternated. Along with Eddie Hapgood were Bill Collier (captain), Jim Imrie (goalkeeper), and forwards Charlesworth, Aitken, Dunsire, Chalmers, Cairns, Starsmore and Pitchford. Cecil Campbell, a superb full back, was an accomplished ballroom dancer who with his wife (née Marshall) won many competitions.

Philip Hague was one of the small boys who used to lie in wait near the old dressing rooms, hoping for the autographs of their idols: "Two of mine were Maurice Dunkley who went on to play for Manchester City and Alec Linnell the 'stopper' centre half who later let me off guard duty in the RAF when he found I was one of his fans. They were worthy successors to the great Eddie Hapgood who played for Arsenal and captained England.''

Maurice Dunkley, a schoolboy footballer who joined the Poppies in the mid-1930s, soon gained a reputation and after a season was spotted by talent scouts, Ted Grove recalls. He was invited to join Northampton FC, and from there signed for Manchester City in exchange for three players and a fee. One of the three who figured in the swap is named by Eric Groome as international centre forward Tilson. Eric says of Dunkley ''In the 1930s he played for Kettering at what was known as outside right. His speed and ability to dribble past defenders had to be seen to be believed. He could tap the ball by the defender's left foot, or sometimes between his feet, skip round the player, and be down the touch line before his opponent could recover.''

Dunkley originally worked and played cricket for Freeman, Hardy and Willis and was invited to turn out for the County in June 1938. He was signed after scoring a half-century at number six, and spent some seasons with Northants. After the war he ended his footballing days with Kettering and Corby.

Well remembered is Jack Starsmore, one of five boys in a Brigstock family. His brothers Ted, Joe, Fred and Jim were all sportsmen playing for local teams. Jack was always an idol with the Poppies – a bustling scorer whose talent took him on to Coventry and Swindon. His nephew Colin kept a record of some of his appearance and scores. In 1925/26 he made 46 appearances and scored 33 goals, in 1926/27 48 appearances and 20 goals, in 1927/28 the figures were 49 and 25, 1928/29 7 and 8, and in 1930/31 44 and 31.

Len Toseland, a good old-fashioned centre forward who joined from Harrowden in December 1938 took over when Maurice Carr was stricken with appendicitis, and made one of the best starts of any striker in the club's history. He nailed up a hat trick in his debut against Biggleswade and three more goals in his next match against Peterborough Reserves. Five goals followed in five matches, and he ended up with 13 in a season which saw Kettering winning the Northants League and knockout cup, the East Midlands League, and three charity cups.

Len signed professional forms and had two trial matches with Exeter City in his first season, one against an Arsenal team including internationals Alf Kirchen and Dennis Compton, but had to go off after cutting his head in a collision.

When he went into the Royal Artillery he took his press cuttings, but had to burn them when he fell into Jap hands at Singapore. For three years he worked on the Burma death railway, compelled to help build the bridge over the River Kwai though suffering from dysentery, beri-beri and malaria. He had an ulcerated leg, his weight dropped to seven stones, and only determination pulled him through. He tried football again after the war, but hung up his boots after breaking down in his comeback game with Wellingborough Town.

Others remembered include Fred ("Tich") Althorpe, Harold ("Towzer") Townsend, and "Bungy" Smith for his method of tackling. He could be relied upon to plunder the ball from the opposition which he did by racing hard to tackle, then with a yard to go dropping on one knee and sliding with a straight leading leg, picking the ball off an opponent's foot with spot-on accuracy, as Dennis Wildman described it. "Tich" was a speedy and skilful left winger who would cross the ball to the mouth of the goal to give forwards ample scoring chances, and his speed combined with very short legs enabled him to get back on his feet in a split second if he went down. Alec Linnell married the daughter of club secretary Frank Summerly, and after retiring from football became famous for his fish and chips.

Besides producing players, Kettering in the 1940s contributed referees, among them Dennis Wildman, who after supervising local matches joined the Football League list as a linesman. Already a referee was Harold Prestige, and other men with the whistle were Freddie Smart, Fred Short and Geoff Hodson.

Ted Grove regrets that after the 1927/28 season the Poppies' gates failed to cover wages and travelling, forcing the directors to leave the Southern League and start afresh in the Northants League. The players were then paid expenses but very little for playing, and in the Supporters' Club centenary record published in 1976 the authors David Buckby and Mick Ward say "Some indication of Kettering's fall from almost national prominence can be gauged from the fact that the actual wage bill for the 1936/37 season was less than £500. Ten years earlier (when the team was nicknamed Bill Collier's Mainly Scottish All Stars) they had been paid seven times as much."

The 1930s depression meant that Kettering had to say goodbye to Bill Collier who moved to Dartford and took them to successive Southern League championships in 1931 and 1932, while Kettering after finishing eighth withdrew from the Southern League after a match with Millwall Reserves drew only 296, believed to be the lowest-ever Southern League crowd. The seasoned players were quickly grabbed by other clubs, leaving David Cairns to act as a father-figure for young recruits.

During those years the ground was really a disgrace because of its contours. There was a steep slope from Cowper Street to Rockingham Road, and another from Britannia Road to the north-west corner. It was so steep as to amaze Peter Wilson of the *Daily Mirror* when he visited it with Crystal Palace in the first round of the FA Cup in 1937. Kettering drew 2-2 with Palace at Selhurst Park, and it was the replay at Kettering that produced such a rib-tickling description from Wilson that it is worth giving in full:

THE RAIN WAS BAD ENOUGH, BUT KETTERING . . . .!

Kettering Town 0, Crystal Palace 4

For years I have managed to fill columns about British heavyweight boxers. I have found *something* to say about all-in wrestling and six-day cycling; in my cub-reporter days I even wrote, with enthusiasm, glowing descriptions of vegetable marrows.

But, strike me silly, this Kettering team has me beat.

In all honesty, I cannot think of a single one of their players who is deserving of a (polite) mention. For sheer fumble-footed incompetency they take the prize crumpet.

It is not to Crystal Palace's credit that they won. If they had not they would have deserved the fate of the building whose name they bear. And unlike it, they didn't produce any fireworks.

I thought we had plumbed the depths of sorry soccer in the first half, when the Palace, playing up a hill that could have been used to test the climbing abilities of cars, scored three goals. But that was nothing. First it rained – rained as though someone was emptying the slops from heaven. This gave Kettering players an excuse for sitting down every time they kicked at the ball – but they had done it just as regularly when there wasn't an excuse.

Then it hailed.

Then two players had a fight.

Then it rained again.

And the drops ran off the end of the nearest linesman's nose in a kind of melancholy torrent. Oh, my purple grief, what a match!

Almost every time that Kettering had a chance to shoot, or on the rare occasions they forced a corner, they kicked behind. And sometimes – not through viciousness but lack of skill – they nearly kicked their opponents there too. They ought to have kicked themselves.

For the Palace, Pritchard, Waldron, Collins and Owen played well – the last two particularly so – and Pritchard, Blackman, Pritchard again and Waldron scored the goals in that order.

The one piece of play which provided me with any enjoyment at all was Blackman's goal. It was a beauty. The ball went from right back Owens out to the right wing where Davis snapped it up, then pushed it across to Gillespie, who finally slipped it for the centre forward to find the net.

Perfect toe-to-toe stuff in which a Kettering player never touched the ball.

Kettering is known by its supporters – yes, they do have them – as "the Poppies." And the well-known football figure who suggested that their theme song should be "Will the Poppies Ever Bloom Again?" was not so far out.

Peter Wilson's sallies were received with baffled rage at Kettering, but the following year he was invited to address a sportsmen's service at Bath Road Methodist Church. Greatly daring, he accepted, and got on well with the footballers.

After the war Mr. W. B. Wright, "the man in the straw hat", who headed a meat products firm, became chairman of the Poppies and tackled the gigantic task of levelling and modernising the ground. Peter Wilson returned, forgiven, to perform the opening ceremony. Ever since then the ground, with excellent drainage, has been regarded as one of the best in the country.

Digging out some information for me, the Rev. Nigel Sands of Newbury, Crystal Palace hon. chaplain and historian, found that once before, in November 1928, Kettering visited Selhurst Park for a first round FA Cup tie, playing Peter Simpson, a Scottish centre forward who so impressed the Palace that they signed him, and he remains their highest-ever goal scorer with 165 league and cup goals from 195 games. Kettering lost 2-0, which finished their Cup run, but in the league they defeated Thames Alliance 10-0.

More highlights in the history of a Club which has always been a live wire come from a full account prepared by Reg Abbott to celebrate winning the Southern League in 1956/57 with Tommy Lawton as player manager.

Founded in 1875, and figuring in half a dozen different leagues at various times, Kettering played first on Eldred's field opposite the police station wearing chocolate and pink striped shirts and blue shorts. From early on they were good enough to stage friendlies with First Division teams, including West Brom, Notts County, Notts Forest and Wolves. The team were professionals, paid 10s a week.

In 1893 they moved to North Park, they won the Midland League in 1895/96, and celebrated Queen Victoria's diamond jubilee in '97 by establishing the Rockingham Road ground. After the Midland League success they joined the Southern League, and membership led to a remarkable home game during which the English Cup was carried round the ground.

It happened like this: In 1901 the last Southern League fixture of the season was with Tottenham Hotspur who had just won the Cup, beating Sheffield United. It was the only time the trophy had gone to a non-League team. Arriving by train from Bolton, Spurs proudly brought the Cup with them.

Kettering met them at the station, took them on a tour of the town by horse brake, lunched them at the Robin Hood in Northall whose host was Kettering centre forward McMain, and then took them on a drive round the villages. The match kicked off at 5 pm, and at the interval Spurs directors walked round the pitch to show the Cup to the crowd. Result was an honourable 1-1.

The team was christened the Poppies in 1907, and was widely known as a nursery for players who went on to first class football. One with an unusual career was local man Herbert Dainty who captained Dundee when they won the Scottish Cup in 1910 and then coached and refereed in South America before retiring to Geddington. 'Smiler' Mabelson, an early player, assisted the team's future in a different way, through his son 'Skinner' and grandson Don who both figured in the side when of age.

After a Central Alliance spell, Kettering were back in the Southern League in 1922/23. They built a new stand, became a limited company, and the Supporters Club was formed, contributing funds and eventually excellent dressing rooms. Among transfers Viner went to Leicester for as much as £1,000. Bill Collier came from Sheffield Wednesday as player manager, and in 1927/28 after a triumphant season the Poppies won the Southern League Eastern Section. It was the best period in their history so far.

A disappointment was failure to get into Division III of the League, but continual upward move of players testified to the team's excellence. Eddie Hapgood went to Arsenal after only six appearances, Jack Starsmore went to Coventry for £500, and after a game with Kettering, Crystal Palace asked for five players –

Tommy Lawton in action. One of the all-time greats, he came to Kettering from Arsenal as player manager amid a storm of publicity, and took the side to the championship of the Southern League in 16 months before moving on to Notts County. He is remembered as a goal-scoring prodigy when centre-forward for England, leading what was possibly the finest-ever forward line, and scoring 22 goals in 23 internationals.

(The Times)

Imrie, Simpson, Dunsire, Barrie, and Charlesworth. A scorer in a schools trial on the ground was young Stanley Matthews. Alex Linnell joined the side, destined to give 17 years service and in one season scoring 54 goals, 41 of them headers.

The 1938/9 season was the best for ten years, the Poppies winning all the competitions they entered except the FA Cup. After the war there was progress on all fronts, including moving 7,000 tons of earth to level the ground. Among signings was Arnold Woolhead, an amateur like Edgar Towell in an earlier generation. Arnold scored a hat trick in his first match, nine goals in an 11-3 win at Morris Motors, and 11 in an 18-0 victory over Holbeach, setting a record.

By 1952/53 Kettering finished fourth in the Southern League, but things slipped in 1955/6, and in a bold move the directors signed Tommy Lawton from Arsenal as player manager. Former Everton and England centre forward, Tommy was one of football's all-time greats. Featured on TV, the signing gained Kettering vast national publicity.

Reg Abbott recalls that this ushered in the stormiest period for the administration but the most successful on the playing side. Lawton insisted on fitness, secured new players, and the Poppies won the Southern League championship in 1956/7, the target Lawton had set himself. He expected to need three or four seasons, but achieved it in 16 months, then going out on a high to become player-manager of Notts County.

Besides the Saturday games, the town had some excellent Thursday teams, drawn from staffs of shops which closed for half-day. Kettering Thursday United played on the town ground, and the Kettering Industrial Co-op FC used the Pytchley Road sports ground. Dennis Wildman remembers that people who helped to make a success of the Thursday United were Don Knight the Wellington Street grocer, "Pecker" Woodward of Learner and Woodward, Ted Lewin of cooked meat fame and Pettifer the hairdresser. In the 1930s the team won the Northants FA Thursday Cup from 40 to 50 competing teams spread over the County from Peterborough to Daventry.

The KICS Thursday side was in the reliable hands of "Masher" Draper and Fred Deeley, and general manager Albert Joyce gave every support. For example, when the team was drawn against Brighton Co-op in the Co-op Shield in 1936 the KICS paid all

expenses. Other Thursday teams were United Counties, Kettering
Police and Kettering Butchers.

Showpiece of the season was on Good Friday when Kettering
Thursday played Kettering Co-op. The game used to be watched
by up to 3,000 people on the town ground at sixpence admission,
and for many seasons Alderman Joyce kicked off and then sat
in the stand with the Co-op managers, all wearing bow ties and
trilby hats. Bert's brother used to come if he could – he was a
director of Arsenal FC.

Also in the stand were many private traders, deadly rivals of
the Co-op in business, but united by their love of football.
Kettering police had some good footballers, usually playing other
police teams on Thursdays, though one or two regularly helped
Kettering Town.

The *Football Telegraph* was an essential feature of Saturday
afternoons including even the smallest teams among its roundup
of results. Dennis Wildman remembers that "after the game
someone would volunteer to cycle with the results and scorers
to the *Telegraph* office for inclusion in the *Pink 'Un*, then price
one (old) penny, with maybe a little report. Some of the
messengers had a job to write, but they would just press the bell
in Dryland Street and tell sports editor Harry Newbould or one
of his chaps about the game, and it would be in that night when
the paper came out about 6.30."

Philip Hague notes that the first halves of the matches were
well reported in the paper, sometimes with pictures of the scorers
(known as "thumbnails" in the office), but with time pressing
the second halves occupied much less space – "My favourite
for brevity was 'In the second half there were many good things.'
I think even Kettering's famous schoolmaster Mr. Kirby would
have been proud of that precis, at any rate for word economy.

"There were characters among the crowd, one of whom would
start shouting 'Time we had one' within a few minutes of kick-
off. And some players were highly original. One side, arriving
by train and being held up at the Furnaces, jumped out, did a
lightning lineside change under the hedge, ran across the
intervening field and trotted on to the ground just in time for
the kick-off."

Phil says that before the reconstruction of the ground the car
park was a field grazed by the horse that pulled the mowing

machine, and Kingsley Avenue residents whose houses backed on to the field were allowed to let their chickens run in it as a "thank you" for not complaining about the gents' loo, close to the boundary hedge.

He has never forgotten Elworthy's advertisement for their Kettering Choice Ales which ran along the canopy of the covered terrace on the Britannia Road side: " 'To toast the victors, to console the vanquished.' What a gentlemanly exhortation. No one likes losing, but I have let the spirit of that advertisement guide me all my life."

A good story about those primitive days comes from Doug Cleaver: "One day when the team were starkers in the crumby hut that passed as a changing room, "Bungy" Smith climbed on to the roof and dropped a handful of fireworks down the stove chimney. One can imagine the alarm and despondency that ensued when the stove erupted in their midst."

Some games produced fireworks. Reported to the Northants FA in 1935 was a fracas at a village derby, when a fight between two players reached the police court. The footballer in the wrong was fined £1, in default 14 days imprisonment, plus £2 2s legal costs.

KETTERING TOWN C.C.

I don't know whether cricket has a patron saint, but back in 1885 Kettering seemed to have one in the making. A lot of the town's sporting stars began to think that Kettering ought to have a town cricket club, and eventually met to form one. Records give the impression that it just happened, but reading between the lines you feel that the moving spirit was a curate at the Parish Church, the Rev. George Thurston. From the parish magazine he seems to have been a lively young man of social standing, and at the inaugural meeting despite the presence of eminent townsmen he was given the honour of proposing the resolution that a Kettering cricket club be formed. So thanks to George bowling the metaphorical first over, Kettering has enjoyed well over a century of excellent cricket down by the Slade.

Though he made a splendid start to his career, George was not one of life's lucky people. He was one of three sons of Old Etonian Charles Thurston of Kew who followed their father to Eton. Frank became a sea captain and Edgar made a medical career in Madras. George after Kettering became curate at Broughton and vicar of Welford, but must have been stricken in health for he never married and was appointed to the tiny parish of Stoke Dry, which had only 54 people. He stayed there for 14 years until he died in 1916 after a six-month illness.

The love of cricket was at a high point when Kettering Town C.C. was founded. Dr. William Roughton, one of the great Victorians, had his own ground in the environs of his house between Northampton Road and Hazelwood Lane, and in a South versus West of England game he persuaded W. G. Grace and Ranjitsinhji to play there. For years there had been many contests between scratch elevens, but it was only when Dr. Roughton and the hard-hitting young curate joined forces that talent was concentrated in a Club that could worthily represent the fast-growing town.

Noted names among the first committee members were H. G. Gotch, J. A. Gotch, and secretary Charles Saunders, an enthusiast if ever there was one. He captained Northants Club and Ground, and as light relief from his architect's practice he would make expeditions to the gasworks field carrying bat, ball and stumps in his cricket bag, and some sixpences in his waistcoat pocket.

On his way Charles would gradually attract a crowd of youngsters alerted by the cricket bag and eager to try conclusions with him. Arrived at the field, he would set up his stumps, put sixpence on the middle one, and invite embryo cricketers to bowl to him. Anyone who knocked out the middle stump got the sixpence (approaching £1 in purchasing power at today's values).

The gasworks field, on the left opposite the gasworks at the bottom of Gas Street, belonged to John Stockburn who let the Club use it for £15 a year, provided his cattle were allowed to graze undamaged. How they were corralled and guarded during matches is not recorded, nor are the comments of mothers and wives who washed the team's whites, but such an arrangement could not last. After a season the Club moved to a field off Headlands belonging to Mr. Manning, a farmer who lived in Tanners Lane.

Some readers will remember that in the 1920s the gasworks field was securely walled and fenced, presumably for the benefit of the Stockburn cattle. When I was a boy I used a cinder pathway that ran along the edge of it, close to the brook, before Northfield Avenue was built. The path was a short cut to save gasworks people the long walk through the town, and they were compelled to keep to it by the head-high diagonal palings of heavy wooden construction with sturdy gates at each end. Even if contemplated, rustling the Stockburn cattle or chasing them for fun would have been far from easy. Gas Street was today's Meadow Road.

After a few years, housebuilding off Headlands compelled a second move, and the Club selected another field deposited by the waters of the Slade brook in ages past. In 1903 it moved to land between Northampton Road and the railway to Cransley Furnaces, bounded on the east by the main line and station, near the town yet secluded and quiet if you discount occasional puffing and whistling from passing trains.

At first rented from the Duke and then bought on mortgage, the ground has been the Club's home ever since. With the addition of the graceful main pavilion designed by J. A. Gotch, a smaller pavilion for a second square, and the gradual development of further sports facilities it made a fine headquarters. Lord Lilford, a great supporter of county and local cricket, gave the pavilion clock to add the final touch. He was a stickler for timekeeping, and may have given the clock as a friendly hint.

Another valuable scenic addition has been the row of 48 poplars, each given by a vice-president. Age has wearied them, the branches becoming brittle, and they have had to be pollarded a couple of times, but they are still a welcome feature supplemented by a second row in 1966. John Larcombe, seeing the ground for the first time, wrote "Like so many newcomers I immediately fell in love with it – the distant views, the lovely trees, the style of the pavilion (still to my mind the most attractive visually in the county), and of course the warmth of the welcome." With such a headquarters the Club rightly claimed to possess one of the foremost Midland cricketing centres.

Sadly Gotch's pavilion was burnt down in the early hours of 16 September, 1996.

Forethought in acquiring so much territory paid dividends, for the club was able to lease a pitch to Kettering Rugby Club, and there was room for two cricket squares after the second war when increasing membership demanded six elevens. Teams fielded every week were three on Saturdays, two and sometimes three on Sundays, and a Thursday XI. Later, forming the Cricket and Sports Club was a welcome move, making full summer and winter use of the ground and enabling sportsmen and women to speak with one voice. Joining forces were the Cricket Club, Men's and Ladies' Hockey Clubs, Skymoons Mixed Hockey Club, Spinney Lawn Tennis Club and the Rifle Club. So much new blood, it was reported, had an enlivening effect on the Cricket Club.

Like many beautiful spots, the ground has a happy aura. Thinking of it my mind goes back to one of those days you always remember, for no particular reason. It was Feast Week in the 1930s. The sun was high in a cloudless sky, the Fair was displaying its pageantry on the "rec" around Thurston's peacocks, and a County match was in progress. I, as a youngster on the *Evening Telegraph*, arrived on an important assignment. Nothing to do with cricket or the fair.

My quest was for one Stainless Stephen, a top-of-the-bill comedian who was watching the match. He was so famous that word of his presence flew round the town, and the editor wanted him interviewed. Looking for Stainless I had to walk round and survey the crowd. The factories were closed and the ground was packed with people, their feet stretched out to the boundary line, enjoying themselves with flasks, bottles, packed lunches, sun hats made from morning papers, and of course the cricket. It was Kettering at its best.

I found Stainless sprawled in a deckchair, minus his trademarks of shining silver waistcoat and tiny bowler hat, but loudly amusing the fans around him. He dictated for me a pungent comment on the game, sprinkled with the commas, semi-colons and full stops that made his act so distinctive, and I departed. I don't remember who was playing Northants (probably Glamorgan, who so often seemed to be the opposition at Kettering), and back at Dryland Street the editor was pleased with Stephen's sallies. Just a vignette. Seeing Kettering folk really happy on a day off made it something for memory's scrapbook.

In the 1920s the County began to see Kettering as a venue for first class matches, and Glamorgan started the ball rolling in 1923. By 1925 Kettering had become so attractive that each season it could claim three county matches, against Yorkshire, Warwickshire and Essex. There was a huge attendance for the Surrey game in 1954 which the then champions won by only one wicket, but by 1970 fixtures outside the county ground were becoming uneconomic, and the axe fell on Kettering for three-day events. John Player one-day league games went on until 1973 when the final county match took place, fittingly against Glamorgan who became both first and last opponents in a half-century of splendid first-class cricket.

The Club marked its 100th year with an excellent centenary book written by members, to which I am indebted. It recalls that Kettering cricket in the 1920s was dominated by the Wrights, the famous sporting and shoe manufacturing family. There were plenty of them, half a dozen played for Northamptonshire, and between them they could field a complete family XI including P. A. Wright, a University and County all-rounder of the highest class. They challenged Kettering Town in 1919 for charity to mark the safe return of members of the family from the war, and won by 107 runs to 70. So many Wrights wanted to take part that the teams had to be XIVs.

A routine specimen of the family's prowess comes from scores reproduced in the book. In a match against Northampton Saints P. A. Wright took six wickets and caught a seventh batsman off Bert Wright's bowling, the Saints making 143 against Kettering's 207 for 6 declared. Top scorers were W. King 52, H. J. H. Lamb 48, Steve Wright 32 and P. A. Wright 28 not out.

Mr. W. O. Tailby of Burton Latimer remembers one season when P. A. Wright did the double, scoring 1,000 runs and taking 100 wickets for the County: "He got the 1,000 runs earlier in the season and in the last match he wanted about four wickets. The captain kept him bowling until he got his 100." It was different for Ken Dix in one of the Kettering Town games when "his anguished groan as he was in his mid-nineties and the skipper called him in and closed the innings" remained in Jim Carr's memory. In the Wright era officials included president Sir Arthur de Capell Brooke, vice-president J. C. Wilson, honorary secretary and treasurer W. H. Cawstin, and captain Bert Wright.

The centenary book records some notable events on the Kettering ground during the county matches era. In 1924 Phil Mead, Hampshire and England opening bat, scored his 100th century. In 1928 Suffolk declared at 571 for 9, helped by Ranji's nephew Duleepsinhji who made 198. In 1933 Northants scored 539 against Essex, but only 27 in their first innings against Yorkshire, which saw Sutcliffe hit 10 sixes during his 113. In 1934 Reg Partridge took 9 for 66 against Warwickshire, and in 1935 Bill Bowes for Yorkshire took 16 for 35 in two Northants innings. In 1936 for Somerset Harold Gimblett made a century before lunch, and in 1939 George Cox Jr. of Sussex knocked up the highest first class score at Kettering – 232.

Dr. Harold Cooper Pretty was outstanding among Kettering players. He was son of Dr. George Wilson Pretty who practised for 36 years at Fressingfield, Sussex, and died in 1883 after a long illness, leaving a widow and six children (besides 10 children by a former marriage) totally unprovided for. He had been a subscriber to the Royal Medical Benevolent College, and Harold was elected a fondationer at Epsom College in 1886 aged 10.

Starting bottom of the class, by the time he left in 1891 he had been elected University College Scholar and Carr Exhibitioner, was captain of cricket, and played rugby and hockey. He played cricket for his Oxford College and for Oxford County, then for Surrey for several seasons, making 124 against Notts at the Oval on August Bank Holiday 1899.

He stood down while training in London hospitals and taking his degree, and after he came to Kettering assisted the Town in half-day games. Then in 1906, called on to play for Northants after seven years away from first class cricket, he put up a sensational performance against Derbyshire at Chesterfield. He scored 200, contributing the lion's share of the 280 total at more than a run a minute during a 3¼ hours innings, thrilling the crowd with many sixes among 35 boundaries.

Dr. Pretty was involved in a tragic accident at the town ground. In 1908 he was practising at the nets and hit a ball which skimmed the dividing net and went on to strike 19-years-old Frank Cedric Page on the temple. Frank had just bowled to the neighbouring batsman, had picked up the ball, and was turning to make his next run-up. Seeing him fall, Dr. Pretty ran to him, and at first Frank said he was not hurt and would carry on. Dr. Pretty took him home to 'Ashburn' in Station Road and called in another doctor and a trained nurse, but the young man died the following afternoon from concussion and haemorrhage. The inquest yielded a verdict of accidental death, and there were many messages of sympathy. The victim had come to Kettering to be articled to Reader Smith, the town surveyor, and was just at the beginning of his career. It was one of the rare fatalities that occur at cricket, and doubly sad that one of the town's doctors should have been involved.

I used to find it hard to reconcile quietly-spoken John Lamb, solicitor and clerk to Kettering magistrates, with his alter ego H. J. H. Lamb, redoubtable hard-hitting batsman and many-handed wicket keeper who was a pillar of town and county cricket. He was of great assistance to the County in the very difficult "lean years" between the wars, making 38 appearances between 1934 and 1938, as captain in the first half of the 1936 season.

Northants, with a great reputation as gallant and sporting losers won only two matches in 1934. H. J. H. played in both, and against

Hampshire at Bournemouth he caught Phil Mead in both Hampshire innings – tit for tat for Phil's 100th century at Kettering. He served Kettering Town as captain, chairman and president, and in his reminiscences singled out Mr. W. C. Farnsworth as one to whom the club owes an inestimable debt as captain in the 1920s, president until 1964, and man of business who negotiated the purchase of the ground and the sale of part of it to the borough, paying off the mortgage.

Among others H. J. H. picked out for yeoman service were the Wrights (Bert he thought the best), captain Walter King who with Edgar Towell made a formidable pair of bowlers, groundsman/professional Meunier whose son Alec played, Reg Partridge whose off-spinners were perfected after coaching from Ben Bellamy, and outstanding players Gordon Sharman and university blue Jimmy Potts, grouped with Joe Shapeira and Brian Reynolds.

Another first class Kettering player who assisted the County between the wars was Maurice Dunkley. A friend, Eric Groome, says of him: "Maurice worked for Freeman Hardy and Willis, and batted at four for them in the Kettering Town League – an attractive fast-scoring front foot batsman with all the shots. I can still see him walking out to bat at the North Park – a stocky figure with blond hair and a quick walk, every inch an athlete. That afternoon he scored heavily with a style and flair that was quite breathtaking to my young eyes. Although largely uncoached he had a natural talent that was clearly destined for higher things.

"In 1937 he was called by the County for a three day match at Kettering, and did well, scoring more than 50. After signing professional forms he played in 36 first class matches between 1937 and 1939. Sadly he was unable to translate his early promise into a successful career at top level, from 64 innings managing only 904 runs. But if he was a natural cricketer who only just missed the big time he was also a natural footballer and realised it." Maurice's career best was at Scarborough in 1938 when he scored 70, partly off the great Verity, and with his captain Robert Nelson adding 102 for the 8th wicket.

The other members of Kettering Town who represented the County up to 1984 are recorded in the Centenary Book as H. C. Pretty 1906-07, S. King 1907-08, A. Wright 1919-20, B. Wright 1919-22, P. A. Wright 1921-29, N. E. Wright 1921-22, R. L. Wright

A youthful picture of John (H. J. H.) Lamb
taken when he was playing for the County
in 1934-38. He was captain for the first
half of the 1936 season, highest score 91.
not out, and kept his hand in during the
war by captaining Southern Command HQ
team. He played for the Town from 1931 to
the 1950s with several seasons as captain,
following college cricket at Cambridge
where he was captain at King's and
country house games for Lord Lilford's XI.
(Edward Lamb)

1923-26, S. Wright 1922-23, G. H. Johnson 1922-32, E. F. Towell 1923-34, H. J. H. Lamb 1934-38, W. R. F. Chamberlain 1946, W. T. Nevell 1946-47, B. L. Reynolds 1950-70. R. Wooster performed the hat trick against Dublin University in 1925. S. A. Leadbetter was on the County staff but did not play in a championship match.

Back to normal after the second war, when it served as a Fire Service station, the Kettering ground again became an attractive venue, and the County invited an Argentine XI, an All-India XI and the Combined Services to play first class matches.

Jim Carr saw the war as a watershed. The fabled Wrights had quit the scene, Edgar Towell lingered for a season or two demonstrating an antique round-arm delivery, and a few like Jack Tebbutt moved philosophically from the pitch to a bench on the boundary. Strengthened by Dick Wooster and a few of his contemporaries, new players were joining, often from far away – Bert Fillingham, Tom Cullen, Dick Popham, Jack Norman, Ted Winsor, Gordon Tye, Peter Lansberry, Keith Arthey, Stan Frost, Martin Sykes, John Brown, Graham Wilson, Michael Duck, Tom Harvey, Jim himself, and many others.

A change in the playing environment came in 1950-51 when the County League was formed. John Lamb says it was no means a foregone conclusion that Kettering would support the project initiated by British Timken under the aegis of Northants skipper Freddie Brown in the hope of finding more talent for the County. Kettering had a very good friendly fixture list which had to be sacrificed when the club joined the league, and some valued fixtures such as Leicester Ivanhoe were lost for ever.

Prominent in forming the league were Gordon Draper and John Larcombe. Gordon was always one of the leading players and skipper of one or other of the Club teams, besides being a champion raiser of funds. John was secretary, chairman, or in charge of the ground for nearly 30 years and with Fred Lawson played a major part in opening up the second square in 1955 after Claude Miller had grubbed out the ancient dividing hedge. Kettering was one of 10 founder clubs in a league which later grew to five divisions with 35 clubs.

John Larcombe had an unusual claim to fame. He made two successive centuries 6,000 miles apart, one of them as an opener, the other batting at number eleven. It happened like this. After coming to Kettering in 1951 and joining the teaching staff at Kettering Grammar School he gravitated to the Cricket Club via the George Hotel, and scored 100 for the Wanderers in his first game.

His previous century in Argentina was more complicated. An Anglican Clergy XI played the British Embassy, the clergy were thin on the ground, and called in John to help. As he was a teacher at St. George's College not in holy orders, it was thought proper that he should go in last. When he reached the wicket the score was 59 for 9, but an hour later the clergy had put on 102 runs of which John had made 101 and the perspiring canon at the other end a single, though he'd done sterling work by keeping his wicket standing.

At KGS John was 21 years in charge of the school's 1st XI, encouraged by headmaster and offspin bowler J. K. Dudley, himself a Wanderers player, and many promising young cricketers were produced. John was elected Kettering Town's first life member and held County appointments including the presidency of the League. At Bristol University he had captained cricket and rugby and played first class rugby for Bristol.

Humorists among centenary writers recall some memorable incidents. Jim Carr never forgot Bill Moore's incredulous cry of despair as the ball bobbed from his hands when Rushden's David Roberts spooned up a dolly (Bill went on to score a century), or the drum-beat on Murray James's chest when an East Carlton skier dropped through his clutches. Or Paddy Adkins "smirking at a pretty girl on the boundary before snorting like a war horse and flinging himself and the ball down the wicket."

*When the cricket pavilion went up in flames many of the Club's
photographs were lost, but this one of the 1954 Wanderers XI has
survived. Members standing (l to r) are F. R. Toseland, J. L. Carr,
P. J. Adkins, J. K. Dudley, W. Green, D. Goss; seated M. R. Walker,
J. R. Larcombe, C. A. Caswell, A. P. Miller (captain), F. S. Harlow,
P. G. Tye, J. V. Deer, and Peter Larcombe, then scorer. Setting shows
the sylvan beauty of the ground which impressed John Larcombe, who
loaned the picture.*

Peter Larcombe, John's son, remembers Reg Lilley passing from
hero to villain by taking five wickets in five balls and then
dropping the catch that would have clinched victory. And Paul
Amos colliding with batting partner Ron Smith, and having the
damage sewn up in the pavilion by Dr. Fred Harlow. Graven on
centenary captain Graham Abbott's memory is the kneeling figure
of Jim Ball banging his head on the ground after missing a simple
catch at gulley. John Larcombe recalls how Aian Bowran bloodied
his face on the fence making a great effort for a catch. Helped
from the arena he was asked if he wanted doctor, dentist or vicar,
and he said he'd sooner see his bank manager. They were all in
the team.

Writing a thumbnail sketch of Gordon Draper, Peter Larcombe
found him an outstanding personality around whom fun
revolved: "He was spreadeagled by a ferocious throw-in at
Harborough. Trying for a slip catch at Burton his trousers fell

102

down. Somewhere else he had to be disentangled from his long-sleeved pullover because of his haste to bowl out a prize 'bunny', and so terrified of him was one batsman that he dropped his bat.'' One Draper tale (he had a repertoire) was about Jack Norman's astonishment when he found a lady using the team's showers. Laughter, they say, was synonymous with the Sunday B team. Amid the laughs, Gordon raised £3,000 for the Club besides scoring a run for each £1 and probably taking more wickets than any other member in history.

Two more in the gallery of fame are Brian Reynolds and Harry Mitchell. Brian, named as the most distinguished among Kettering-born cricketers made over 21,000 runs for the County and scored one of his 21 centuries in his benefit match against Leicestershire.

Harry Mitchell for 25 years captained the Thursday XI, never missed a catch all that time, filled the jobs of captain, convenor and caterer, and hit a 50 on his 50th birthday, Jim Carr says.

Jim scored his final century at 57, and when he became a successful author carried his love of cricket into his books. One reviewer hailed the description of a game in *A Season in Sinhji* as the best ever written, and Jim had the distinction of reviewing cricket books for Wisden, lunching in the hallowed Long Room at Lord's. He fills in lots of Kettering memories. Bill Moore was the Club's first rugby international, before Nick Drake-Lee, and Fred Lawson, Grammar School chemistry master and many years Wanderers' umpire had his individual way of explaining his lbw decisions to batsmen at the bar afterwards. Dry comments from treasurer George Drever and Charlie Caswell always enlivened the scene, and Jim never forgot glimpses of two people. One was Dick Curtis passing by with his cricket bag the year he was captain – the first Club member Jim saw – and the other Keith Arthey serenely watching one of his sixes dropping behind an Earls Barton hedge.

Jim observed Mr. Mills, the last full-time groundsman ''wintering it out, crouched before a single-element heater'', rounding off John Lamb's recollection of Mr. Meunier, the Club's groundsman/professional in the 1920s, a useful all-rounder whose son Alec later played for Kettering. As long ago as 1885 the Club had its own professional, Mr. H. Panter of Desborough.

When Allah Buksh came to Kettering in 1939 as a schoolboy

evacuee he had a prompt introduction to cricket. Syd and Lou Richards with whom he was billeted were captain and scorer of the Oakley Street Fuller Mission team, and one of his earliest memories was a game at Cranford, a village linked with the Town C.C. as the Rev. Sir Frederick Robinson when squire was a founder vice-president. Allah joined the Casuals, based at the Waggon and Horses off Northall. Then he worked for a year at Mobbs and Lewis, serving as cricket team secretary and enjoying the privilege of riding the works bike with a kitbag full of bats and stumps strapped to the front carrier. With no gears it is not surprising that Allah arrived at a Cransley game a little fatigued, helping with the meagre 34 runs the Mobbs team scored in two innings: "It didn't matter – we were happy with the pre-match pints, skittles in the Three Cranes, and the splendid tea provided. After more pints in the evening none of us could remember which way we cycled home. In 1948 there was not one internal combustion engine among the lot of us – so different from today when with easy travel one hears of the occasional village team which hasn't a single member from its village." Another cycling cricketer, Jim Carr, asks "Whatever happened to the Colts? Norman Hardy and I used to take nine lads on bicycles to play against men's sides like Rushton."

Rushton provides the ending for this chapter. In 1935 its Rector, the Rev. K. C. Horwood, to brighten up village cricket, promised batsmen ten shillings (a lot of money then, buying almost £50 worth today) for every 50 scored within 45 minutes, and £1 for every century scored within 90 minutes. I don't remember anybody winning the money.

And in 1906, which may make up for there being no mention at all so far of ladies' cricket, Miss E. Wetherall, daughter of an earlier Rushton rector, formed a ladies' team. They played Miss Vials' team of lady cricketers. Miss Wetherall scored 45 not out, and took 9 for 21, while her sister Miss M. Wetherall was not out 51.

To see how they would get on against a male XI, they went to the County Ground to meet Master R. Dale's XI, which included several public schoolboys.

The Dales declared at 268 for 5, and the ladies replied with 237, an excellent score considering the hampering effect of the long skirts worn in those days. So there!

After writing this chapter I found some notes about Stainless Stephen's visit. The match, on the day of Kettering Feast, was a remarkable one for the wrong reasons, marking the least fortunate point of Northamptonshire cricket. The visitors were Yorkshire. Bill Bowes took eight Northants wickets for 18. Four Northants wickets went for nine. They scored only 62, and Yorks went ahead to win by an innings and 166. Stainless observed ''You don't want me to say anything funny. The cricketers have done it.'' The year was 1935.

130 YEARS OF RUGBY

Born of soccer, which it found boring, the rugby game behaved as rebellious offspring always will, defying its parents' rules and doing the opposite. It demanded tackling that brought opponents crashing to the ground, promoted boot-milling hurly-burlies of muscular strife every few minutes, changed the goal posts into gallows, maltreated the spherical ball, and elevated picking up and carrying to a fine art. At first the teams were 20-a-side, roughness was encouraged, and rugger was certainly not a game for the puny.

Kettering was ahead of the times, taking up rugby before the formation of the Rugby Union in 1871 when the game was in the wilderness. It dated from 1823, when at Rugby School William Webb Ellis brightened up a dismal soccer match by picking up the ball, running with it, and touching down at the opposite end.

Though severely censured, he had started something, and the idea of a strenuous new game caught on. The next 48 years saw varying versions played to local rules in different parts of the country. Uppingham School had its own rules, and the first Kettering games, by way of experiments, conformed to the Uppingham code.

Credited with pioneering rugby in Kettering is the Rev. the Hon. John Marsham, rector of Barton Seagrave when Lady Hood was living at the Hall. Kettering RFC has thoughtfully prepared a history of its first 100 years, edited by Tony Hewitt, to which I am indebted. It introduces the rector as an example of muscular Christianity who played cricket for the County and was 'father of a dozen or so children.''

This was correct as far as it went, for the rector and his wife had five boys and six girls, and seven servants to look after them. He came of a distinguished family originating at Stratton Strawless in Norfolk, was grandson of the Duke of Buccleuch through his mother, the fourth daughter of the fourth Duke, and was second son of the third Earl of Romney. A Cambridge BA, he spent 40 years at Barton, where the patron was his grandfather, leaving in 1908 for Haccombe, Devon, and living on until 1926 when he was in his eighties.

Helping him to start rugby in Kettering were the local cricketers who formed a side, and in a field off Warkton Lane played a team invited by Marsham. The game was under Uppingham rules because at that time the Uppingham School team was captained by Harry Lindsay, eldest son of the Rector of Kettering, Canon Lindsay.

The match led on to many friendly games in which players developed their skills, and Kettering RFC was formed in 1875, playing its first game opposite the London Road brickyard, near where Silverwood Road now stands. Details are not to hand, except that George Roughton was captain, possibly as a compliment to his father who owned the field. No one could have guessed that in the far future the Club would be so successful that it would be able to move to the brickyard and build a fine headquarters on the site.

With plenty of talent to draw upon, the Club built up such a reputation that founder-member C. Farey Mobbs wrote "Kettering was a very powerful amateur side, playing only first class teams and having to go as far as Rugby, Leicester, Birmingham, Stony Stratford, Marlborough and Oundle to find worthy opponents." Home games were played on Eldred's field, a verdant expanse later covered by York and Tennyson Roads, which Green Lane overlooked, hence its name. Building forced the Club to move to land off Gipsy Lane, and then to Bayes Field, off the present Northfield Avenue.

Leading players were Jack Saddington, Miller Wilson, the four Henson brothers, Fred East, Sam Bell, Charlie Dixon, Goss Clarke and Teddy Woolstone. Bushy beards and combination-like shorts gave the team a forbidding appearance.

In the 1890s the Club disbanded due to lack of support – soccer was calling the tune – but by the early 1900s Frank Mobbs was leading a revival helped by the Rev. Grant and the Rev. Lethbridge, John Bond, Arthur Nicholson, Laurence Gotch and brothers Sam and Tom Wallis, playing on Mr. Grundy's field near the golf links and the Church Institute field. Alas, rugby failed again owing to the predominance of soccer, and had to wait until after the 1914-18 war for its second resurrection.

This was led by Irving Bond, son of town clerk John Bond, jointly with 'Bazzer' Bates at a meeting at the Royal Hotel in March 1921 with Frank Mobbs as chairman. Bond and Bates became joint secretaries, Gordon Scott treasurer, and players included O. J. Hargreaves (captain), J. Stanbury, T. I. Bond, W. P. Nutt, H. Borsberry, P. Wallis, F. R. Bates, L. M. Gotch, S. Wright, S. Cattell, C. D. Brown, F. Norton, C. Caswell, L. F. Hales, T. Bye and A. L. Jones (vice-captain).

For some years, when W. C. Farnsworth was president of both outfits, the revived Club played as guests of the Cricket Club at the Northampton Road ground, and then moved to Headlands. Changing and bathing was at the Royal Hotel, and transport was an assortment of old buses and cars, including Jack Linnell's bright red 1923 racing Alvis. The Alvis formed the basis of many mobile tableaux which the RFC entered in carnivals, and at times Norman Tozer used to stand on the bonnet with ropes round the front bumper pretending to "drive" it. Since Jack passed on the car has entered into the care of Bobby Wicksteed, a fellow rugger player and engineer who has lovingly restored it. Though built for lightness, its chassis is so rugged that Jack piled the whole team on board once when the coach broke down.

Through the years many young players were produced by the Grammar, Central and Stamford Road Schools. Dougie Dunmore played when only 13. He had 3d a week pocket money when match fees and travelling expenses came to 1s a week. Match fees were always a problem in the bad years of unemployment and they were tactfully subsidised at times. George Wager says that young players were always teetotal at first because they could not afford both beer and a game of rugby.

Nobody seems to have written the Central School story from the inside, but the Grammar School farewell volume devotes plenty of space to football. I was there when the school still played soccer, and was instructed in it by Vere Parker, then told to forget the little I'd learnt and to switch to rugby instead.

That was in 1921, when as its farewell to soccer KGS won 11 out of 12 matches in the Christmas term, the odd one out being against the staff.

Rugger was played for the remaining 70 years of the school's life, often to major effect, for in 1947 the 1st XV was defeated for the first time in three years, ending a record of 41 consecutive wins. Joe Ashworth, sports master at KGS, was at the height of his success as a wing forward for Kettering RFC in 1931. He kicked more goals than anyone in the Club's history, and twice made nine conversions in one game.

John Wood, Latin master at KGS, went down in KRFC history as one of its finest centre-threequarters ever, George Wager recalls. Wood was a double blue at Cambridge, and other masters who assisted the School team when it met clubs as distinct from rival schools were 'maths' Hopkins, 'history' Woodward and 'science' Hum.

The spartan reputation of rugby entailed ordeals off the field as well as on it. Bathing at the Royal, in the disused stables, was primitive. First came immersion in a barrel of none-too-hot water, then a shivering run to the changing room during which the player was doused with a bucket of cold water. Members reflected enviously on the arrangements at Magdalen College, Oxford, where they could drink a tankard of ale while reclining in a proper bath.

Some 'facilities' endured on away games were even more primitive than Kettering's. At Bedford each player had to wash in a tin bath with a two-gallon kettle of hot water. At Long Buckby the bath was described as a sort of fish tank. Players had to climb up outside and drop in, and visiting clubs used jokingly to complain that they lost a lot of little fellows in its murky depths.

On-field running repairs were in rough and ready hands. Trainer Maycock believed that cold water down the back of the neck could cure anything. He was rivalled by another holder of the office, Bill Marlow, who made diabolical-smelling liniment, and finished off treatment by a quick rub-down with bristly horse-grooming gloves.

Strict requirements ruled members' social lives. Every Saturday afternoon and evening during the season had to be sacrificed to the game, and if any member dared to take his wife or girlfriend out on a Saturday he would find himself kicked out of the team the next week.

When its HQ was at the Royal the club developed an affectionate bond with the landlady, Mrs. Evans, who became the members' unofficial mother. Known as Ma, she was over six feet tall,

Pre- and post-1939 War pictures of Kettering Rugby Club. So few players returned at first that the club was barely able to field one XV, but eventually it fielded five teams. Members in the pictures are: Top photograph 1938-39 – Back row: G. Wallington, A. Walker, B. Jamieson, N. Chambers, A. Panter, G. Dawson, A. E. Smith, D. Panter, B. White (Hon. Sec.). Front Row: J. Giles, N. Andrews, R. Wilson, J. H. Cheaney (Capt.), G. B. Wager, N. Dickerson, A. Wager.

Bottom photograph 1947-48 – Back row: Ref., D. Panter (mufti), M. Green, J. Giles, J. Loake, G. Drake, J. Chaplin, R. Jacques, A. Lawrence, H. Perkins. Front row: J. Tyson, – . Everard, J. Farrow, R. Bainbridge, G. B. Wager (Capt), T. Smith (capped for England against Wales), R. Wicksteed, J. Cosby. The cricket pavilion in the background was burnt down in 1996.   (George Wager)

weighed 14 stones, and could have given a good account of herself if ever called upon to act as chucker-out.

Such tactics were never necessary. One look from Ma was enough. Peter Wilson wrote of her: "We regarded her with a mixture of respect and genuine fear." He had worked up from junior player to president, an office in which he followed his father, J. C. Wilson, and to him fell the daunting task of negotiating with Mrs. Evans on occasions when members' behaviour met with her disapproval.

They must have been rare, for the centenary book records that Club and hostess maintained a smooth working relationship: "She was jolly good to us. She ruled with a rod of iron, but she was kind, tolerant and generous, and put up with a good deal.

"When the annual dinner came round she would take all the surplus furniture out of the dining room and all the pictures off the walls so that if we did start throwing things more solid than bread rolls it would not matter.

"She was thoroughly broad-minded, and after we'd eaten she would stand with the waitresses and listen to Jack Linnell singing rugby songs and enjoy it. Towards the end of the evening most of us would be under the table, but I remember one guest riding a bike on the table among the empty glasses and coming to grief when he tried to turn at the end.

"If things got a bit too outrageous we would always go in and apologise to Ma the next morning, and all would be well. We lost count of the number of times we had to go and make our peace with her."

Mrs. Evans was always anxious to prevent youngsters from making fools of themselves. To keep beer consumption in check, if anyone among the younger element seemed too flush with cash on a Saturday night, she would take most of it off him and return it next morning.

The Royal was highly respectable. If a girl went in and sat in the corridor, Ma would ask if her mother knew she was there. If the answer was No, she would be sent home to tell her mother where she had been. If the answer was Yes, Mrs. Evans would tell her she wasn't the sort of girl she wanted in the place.

Though never used and unknown to most people, her first name was Julia, appropriately of Roman derivation for the discipline she imposed would not have disgraced one of the legions, though she would probably have stopped at decimation – just. Peter Wilson had a highly uncomfortable memory of one occasion when he was summoned to appear before her. A party of members who had been to a game at Wellingborough called in for a drink at the rival George Hotel on the way back. This act of flagrant disloyalty came to Julia's ears, and PW was blamed for it. He emerged chastened, and such a thing never happened again.

Away from the Royal, she was known for her kind deeds. Dougie Dunmore recalled that she had a house at Rothwell, and during the depression allowed hard-hit people to live there rent free.

When Ma left the Royal the pendulum swung to the George, which became the HQ, and Mr. and Mrs. Freddie Sykes are affectionately remembered. Says Dave Buckby: "My era was weaned on Bass from the George. Mr. Sykes was the most tolerant man in the world. With the advent of our own clubhouse it was envisaged that we would all go down there to drink, but things turned full circle when we were driven back by the disco, and all the old sweats went drinking at the George again."

The Club closed down during the 1939 war, and when things returned to normal Bert White, Ralph Bainbridge, Harold Perkins, George Wager and Denis Panter took the lead in getting going again. Bainbridge was 1st XV captain for several years during which the team went 52 games without defeat – half of one season, the whole of the next, and half the following one. In 1948 Kettering Grammar School Old Boys closed down and almalgamated with the Club, with post-war captain George Wager and Denis Panter guiding the absorption. The centenary record says:

"The team of 1954 was really something – prop forward Alan Jenkinson, hookers Tom Loasby and Trevor Smith, Joe Collinson in the second row. Duncan Bennie and Bill Moore two very good scrum halves, Bainbridge full back, and John Chaplin, Noel Henson and Ron Jacques at threequarters showing outstanding tackling – nothing got past them."

Cash and cars were scarce, and Hannington coaches used to transport the team, who would get out and push if there was a temporary breakdown. The favour was returned when they were a man short and the coach driver agreed to act as substitute: "He had never played in his life, so we put him at number eight and told him that if the ball came his way he must put his foot on it and kick it back whence it came. He did this with such enthusiasm that he kicked our scrum half under the chin,'' Ralph Bainbridge remembered.

There were three internationals – Nick Drake-Lee, capped eight times, Bill Moore, and Trevor Smith.

Denis Panter's main playing career covered 34 years from the 1930s when on one occasion though a spectator he turned out for Wellingborough RFC when they were a man short in the Hospital Cup, and scored the winning try. After Kettering closed down in 1939 he used to bike to Corby to play for Stewarts and Lloyds, when Kettering started up again he played for them until 1970 when he was 50, and he turned out for the Veterans against Wellingborough when he was 59. On the admin side he served Kettering as treasurer, secretary, chairman and president, and as the longest serving player he gradually worked down from the 1st XV to the 5th.

The most enterprising move the Club made was in 1960. John Tilley found that the old brickyard in London Road needed a new use, and the committee decided to obtain the site for a ground and headquarters.

The brickyard stood, a dominant group of circular brick buildings and high chimneys, on the left of London Road at the point where you begin the climb up to Wicksteed Park. I suppose I am one of the few people who remember the brickyard when it was still making bricks for local buildings. The clay was excavated on the site and mixed to a marzipan consistency. It was then extruded from a brick-sized orifice and cut off into lengths by a hand-operated wire, as in cheese-cutting. The embryo bricks were then stacked in the kilns and fired. There were three circular kilns, each with a chimney.

Kettering had three field days in March 1938 when the chimneys were felled, each execution attracting a big crowd of spectators. Men with pick and shovel cut out a big C-shaped cavity in the base of each when its turn came, but I do not recall that the chimney was propped up by baulks of timber which were then burnt to allow it to fall, as in the TV chimney-felling series. My mental picture is that the chaps just went on pecking away until a hollow cracking noise warned them to get out, and they ran for it as the chimney fell along the desired line.

This meant that years later the Club was faced with a dreadful site on which to build, consisting of old claypits, bricks, stones and rubbish. Luckily time and talent was at hand among the members. Jim and Duncan Bennie with their earth moving equipment levelled the site, and Tony Hadden designed the building which was opened on 5th September 1963. Tony recalls that up to the start of the first match members were still hand-picking stones out of the pitch. In 1973 squash courts were added., and in 1975 the training ground was equipped with floodlights.

Many good stories form part of club lore. Returning from a game with Magdalen College very late at night, some members stopped at a country pub where the landlord and his wife offered them bed and breakfast free if they would sit up for a while and play them at cards. Nothing is said about who won, but the team members eventually retired and did not sleep well as the beds were damp. Rising next morning for their "free" breakfast they found they had been handsomely duped. The "landlord" and his "wife" had fled, leaving the rugger men to settle all bills. No explanation of the fraud was ever forthcoming.

Geoff and Jack Linnell, who had their own aircraft, were flying back from Belgium to take part in a match at Brighton, but got caught in fog over the town. They made a forced landing on the beach, which caused a minor sensation. Jack cut his knee, but was able to play, to the disappointment of reserve Billy Marriott who was hoping to get a game. Dyker Thew of the *Evening Telegraph* who had just transferred to a new job at the *Brighton Argus*, saw the emergency landing, recognised Jack and Geoff, and in a few minutes had a good story running in his new paper.

To raise cash for the new brickyard HQ, Denis Panter and Noel Henson had the bright idea of winning and selling off a Ford Anglia offered as first prize in a Lowestoft contest. Entrants had to buy a ticket, forecast the number of crans of fish that would be unloaded at Lowestoft on a certain day, and the nearest would be the winner.

Denis and Noel did some research, bought £300 worth of tickets and spent evening after evening filling in forecasts of fish, entering the contest under the name Henter. Their gamble came off, they won the car, and sold it for £500.

A Ford Anglia featured in another achievement, at Sevenoaks on an Easter tour in 1950. Mervyn Jones packed 17 into his car, taking the whole team from hotel to ground in one trip.

Boxer Dixon broke both ankles jumping off a barn at Bennie's farm. At first the injuries were not fully appreciated, and taking him away by car his mates first decanted him in Rothwell Road, saying "If you can walk we'll take you home to Brigstock. If you can't, we'll dump you at the Hospital." Hospital it was.

The game has developed its own philosophy, outlined by members in the centenary book: "Rugby is the finest freemasonry in the world. It is a fantastic game in which you can knock hell out of each other for 80 minutes and then be the best of friends at the bar. It breaks down barriers and cuts across classes, so that any young man who is decent in his own right and can play a hard game will get on well.

"Rugby points to wider horizons, helps one to take life's knocks without getting uptight, and teaches right from wrong, as although rugby players are often accused of tomfoolery, it is nothing more than that. There are always older players about to get a grip and put the brake on, so that youngsters learn in a convivial manner. You never get the sort of loutish behaviour seen in other walks of life."

AN AMAZING URBAN COUNCIL

I wonder how many of my generation, walking about hale and hearty, owe our long life to the old Kettering Urban Council which ran the town from 1894 to 1938? It was famous for fighting childhood diseases which in those days might easily have killed or maimed us.

The 27 members with their officers were an amazingly efficient body based in makeshift buildings around the town. The clerk's department was in Huxloe Place, the surveyor's in the Old Grammar School in Gold Street, the medical officer occupied the Manor House, and the treasurer was above Burton's in Silver Street. They supplied Kettering with nearly all the essential services without which it would have come to a halt – electricity, water, sewage disposal, education, streets and pavements, public health services, fire brigade, housing, planning, general and cattle markets, public library, museum, art gallery, infectious hospitals (with neighbouring councils), the cemetery and planning the crematorium. Only gas came from a private company.

With so much responsibility the council was often under pressure as in the 1933-5 drought when we had to drink the Wicksteed Lake, but it never lacked compassion. Examples were its outstanding work for maternity and child welfare, with the problems of infectious diseases, and the 'white scourge' of tuberculosis.

Various Acts made public health increasingly the concern of local government, and the urban council accepted them with such eagerness that it was always in the lead, either adopting Acts on the first day or introducing measures in advance of legislation. John Burridge, on behalf of town clerk John Chaston, summarised its work for posterity, and I am indebted to him for these facts.

On New Year's Day 1907 the council was able to appoint its first health visitor and sanitary inspector with power to enter factories and workshops to check on conditions for women employees. Houses, too, could be entered to inquire about infant deaths, or to examine children for infectious diseases.

This job, needing delicacy and determination, was one for a woman, and Lancashire lass Annie Townend of Preston, fresh from four years' training was appointed. She was so vigilant that despite infectious outbreaks she brought the infant death rate down to the lowest then recorded, 88.1 per 1,000 live births. This was far too many, but the reason was obvious when the council adopted the Notification of Births Act, 1908. Women were giving birth without a doctor because they could not afford one, but from then on as health visitor Annie was required to step in with advice and help. She was rivalled by her successor Ethel Cohen, who after an unlucky three years which cost five maternal lives brought the infant death rate down to 81.7 in 1914, another record.

Meanwhile, pressing on with improvements, the council started a school canteen for poor children, began school medical examinations, laid in supplies of diptheria anti-toxin, and opened a school clinic. Dr. John Allison working part time, dentists Alfred Leyton and Harry Sturton, and nurse Rose Allen looked after the patients.

A bold move in 1913 was establishing the Open Air Recovery School, one of the country's first in a small town, for 40 defective children, 40 delicate ones, and 20 pre-tubercular youngsters. The £3,000 bill can be multiplied by 100 to give a rough idea of today's cost. A disinfecting and cleansing station was opened for slum children, and to arrange help for overburdened mothers a few ladies met informally and floated the idea of a maternity centre.

The ever-willing Dr. Allison gave his services to the centre before leaving to serve in the war, so that the initial attendance soon outgrew the volunteers and they had to ask for help from the council. It provided a health visitor and premises in School Lane, creating a fully operational infant welfare centre two years before the Act giving these powers.

When more than 200 infants with their mothers were attending in 1919, a second centre had to be opened in Brook Stret. On the wall the organisers found T. C. Gotch's picture "Madonna of the Mount", given by the Industrial Co-op Society in appreciation of their work.

Developments were unceasing. In 1921 the council arranged a hospital scheme for children with orthopaedic trouble, plus dental care for expectant mothers and pre-school children. The first Health Week, publicising all this work, came in 1923, and a blessing to many anxious mothers-to-be followed in 1926 when hospital in-patient benefits were extended to all who could not safely or suitably give birth at home.

Beacon's Gleam, a summer school on the Norfolk coast, was established in 1926 to give seaside holidays to Open Air School pupils and other delicate children, an organiser was engaged for physical training and remedial exercises, a clinic was opened for young orthopaedic patients, and in 1928 the whole town rallied round to form a child welfare voluntary committee recruited from all the women's organisations.

Infant welfare became a national concern under the lead of Lady Astor, the first woman MP, who gave the Astor Shield for a national contest to find the local authority doing the best work. Kettering beat the whole country three years in succession, winning the shield for keeps. The council replaced it with the Kettering Shield, but when the war came the contest ended and the trophy disappeared. It made a surprising and unexplained reappearance in Kettering, Jamaica, in the 1970s.

For years town doctors served as part-time medical officers, but with rising health standards a full time MO for Kettering was needed, and Dr. Cecil Hogg was appointed in 1930. With increasing work, Dr. Florence Bentham was selected as his deputy in 1936, and the health visitors/nurses under the council were increased to six.

To spread benefits more widely, the council arranged with the Nursing Association for children with measles, whooping cough, diarrhoea, pneumonia and ophthalmia to receive free care if parents could not afford payment. It extended maternity benefits to the villages jointly with the County Council. It appointed a consultant obstetrician for difficult cases, and in 1934 with attendances at the clinics almost 10,000 it opened a new welfare centre.

A dramatic new move in maternity care in sparsely-motorised 1938 was the creation of a flying squad based at the hospital, ready to take a consultant obstetrician, a nurse, and emergency equipment anywhere in the district at any time in answer to a doctor's call. Should more than care at home be needed, the St. John volunteered to provide a back-up ambulance.

In the shadow of approaching war the council continued the good work, announcing reduced rates for children's necessities and dentures for expectant and nursing mothers, and recorded lectures for maternity classes. Equipment for the care of premature babies was installed at the hospital, but maternity admissions were limited as the hospital stood by to receive war wounded.

Final improvements during the war were the establishment of a nursery for children whose mothers were on war work, and the introduction of home helps in 1943.

As the changeover to the NHS approached, final statistics showed the success of the council's 40 years work. Health visitors, dealing with only 376 calls in 1907, found their visits totalling 12,710 in 1941, the busiest year, though birth totals remained almost unchanged, 692 in 1907 compared with 726 in 1947. Deaths of mothers fell to nil in the five years 1943-7, and deaths under one year declined to 13 in the 1930s compared with 121 in 1911.

Annual reports reveal signs of the times. In 1909 Dr. Allison complained that there was no one in authority to see that children sat down to canteen meals with clean hands and faces. He took on the job himself, explaining about germs to the children, and cleanliness improved. The doctor followed this up by recruiting lady volunteers to keep order and instruct in table manners.

Less popular was his disapproval of a custom which is still today a source of family pride and pleasure. Youngsters were awarded splendid medals for a completely unbroken school attendance record, but Dr. Allison saw the danger that rather than lose their medal children might go to school when ill, endangering their health and spreading infection, so after 1911 the council ceased to issue the medals.

The best story, typical of the times, its essentials handed down by word of mouth, is about the Ronald Tree Nursery School, established in 1934. Ronald Tree, wealthy MP for Market Harborough, lived at Kelmarsh Hall and when Parliament was sitting commuted by train from Kettering. One day he returned in the same compartment as Mrs. Frances Clarke, chairman of the child welfare voluntary committee. She combined considerable charm with an active zeal for the latest project – a nursery school to be built entirely by voluntary contributions.

During the 100-minute journey she aroused Ronald's interest

Councillor Frances Clarke (right), president of the Maternity and Child Welfare Committee, was in the same train compartment as Ronald Tree (left), millionaire MP for Market Harborough. She told him of Kettering's efforts to found a voluntary nursery school and before the journey ended Ronald had promised the school to the town. (Michael Tree and Kettering Council)

to such an extent that by the time they reached Kettering he had virtually made the project his own, promising to build the school at his own expense, and launch it. He was as good as his word, and came to open it.

This generous gesture was typical. He was a remarkable man, born to wealth and station, with many influential friends in Britain and America, and constantly seeking ways to do good. His descent was American, his businessman father serving as US ambassador to Brussels and St. Petersburg and his great-uncle as ambassador to Rome. Both his wives were American-born, one the niece of Lady Astor. In the 1914-18 war he served as a US pilot, going on raids in tiny aircraft and tossing out bombs the size of cricket balls.

But despite his American origins he was essentially English. He was born here, went to Winchester, developed a great love of country life, and renting Kelmarsh was twice elected MP for Market Harborough, serving from 1933 to 1945. He was parliamentary private secretary to three Ministers of Information – Lord Reith, Duff Cooper and Brendan Bracken – and after seeing the Nazis at close quarters in Germany in 1934 he became anti-appeasement and pro-rearmament, working for the establishment of Winston Churchill as prime minister.

Between 1940 and 1942 Ronald Tree and his wife Nancy assumed a great responsibility and privilege. Chequers, the prime minister's country retreat, was a prime target for German bombers and could not be used, but a safe refuge out of London was needed. So, when away from Downing Street, Winston Churchill, his family, distinguished guests, his entire staff and communications facilities, with troops to guard them, were sheltered in conditions of great secrecy hosted by the Tree family at Ditchley Park, Oxfordshire, a beautiful house and estate which the Trees bought when they left Kelmarsh.

Throughout the war Ronald worked tirelessly in Britain and the US to improve relations and secure financial aid, and when peace came he returned to Barbados, living between his home at Heron Bay and New York. His leadership and benefactions included donating cricket grounds which helped to produce formidable West Indian players, and earned him the nickname of "King of Barbados."

When the nursery school reached its diamond jubilee in 1994 his son Michael agreed to attend the celebrations, and a mayoral reception was arranged, but Michael was compelled to telephone his apologies. Says governor Mrs. Anita Holt: "He was on the Kettering train in St. Pancras, but a bomb scare prevented it from leaving. While our celebrations were in full swing, he was imprisoned in a sweltering railway carriage. It was a great disappointment."

After Ronald Tree died in 1976, *The Times* said: "He had a genius for friendship. Except for Churchill, he was the most effective British official associated with Anglo-American public relations up to Pearl Harbour."

We should cherish the Ronald Tree School. It commemorates a great and modest man to whom the nation owes more than we realise.

Back now to paragraph 3, when we drank the Wicksteed Lake in the dreadful drought of 1933-5. Thorpe and Cransley reservoirs were both dry, and I was one of the many people who walked about on their sun-baked beds of cracked mud. It was a very serious emergency for Kettering, as the two reservoirs were practically the only sources of supply of town water.

John Burridge records that after an almost rainless 1933 the reservoirs were very low through the winter, and in January 1934 mains water had to be rationed. It was turned on for 13½ hours a day, and in February for only 10½ hours. The council, seriously alarmed, surveyed its area to find wells, streams and rainwater cisterns suitable for uses other than drinking or cooking. They were all inspected by the medical officer, and notices were displayed specifying their permitted use.

By May, as no rain had come, mains water was turned on for only 5½ hours in the 24, and in July the ration was cut to three hours. The Wicksteed Lake was pressed into use as a last resort, and the town survived on its water, taken via surface mains laid along Windmill Avenue to Clover Hill for filtering and chlorination. When the rains eventually came, Col. J. P. Haugh, the town's surveyor and engineer, and the public health staff emerged from the ordeal with flying colours. Not a single case of disease had been attributable to unsafe water.

A lesser emergency occurred in 1944, when mains water was off for 12 hours during the night from 1 March to 31 November. These crises hastened the formation of the Mid-Northamptonshire Water Board in 1949, and ultimately Anglian Water.

Many well-remembered names figure among the full time and long service public health staffs – Drs. C. B. Hogg, Florence Bentham and J. V. L. Farquhar; Mr. J. P. Finnan, school dentist; Mr. H. E. Deuce and Frank Drury, sanitary inspectors; Geoffrey Walshaw and Brian Hodgins, public health inspectors; Harry Taylor, nuisance inspector; Misses E. E. Ewing, Hannah Ryding, Gertrude Barrett, H. B. Schofeld and L. McCaffrey (Mrs. Ambrose), health visitors/nurses; and Dora Spencer, medical clerk who served for 41 years. John Burridge ran her close with 40 years as chief clerk in the public health department and senior administration assistant in the borough secretary's department, including war service.

Others who figured for shorter periods included Dr. W. Drake-Lee, medical officer; Mr. Salisbury and Mr. Robert Watson, consultant obstetricians; Mr. E. A. Lawson and Dr. F. Wilson-Stuart, orthopaedic surgeons, Mr. E. Harries-Jones, ophthalmic surgeon; Mr. N. E. Kendall, aural surgeon and Mr. Trevor Spencer, vet, dairies and cowsheds, all serving part-time; Miss M. Crombie, nurse/health visitor; Eva Dyson, dental assistant; Miss Boardman and Miss F. E Udell, school nurses; Miss M. E. Harrison and Miss W. J. Blanchard, physical training; Elsie Bicheno speech therapist; John Barritt, nuisance inspector; and Bertie Clarke, rat catcher.

The good they did lingers on.

In the last-chance saloon as this book appears is the fine old stone-built factory in Northall Street. Despite Civic Society efforts to save it, its destruction is planned to make way for commercial units. One of the town's first purpose-built factories which originally made corsets, it is among Kettering's dwindling number of architectural exclamation marks, and the Robin Hood next door has its moments – see 'The Soccer Scene.' Required is someone with enlightenment and cash to act as saviour and find new uses for them. (George Morgan)

Index to
Old Kettering –
A View from
the 1930s
Book 5